What people are saying about

Phantoms in the Night or ETs?

Our awareness of flying saucers and alien beings first shot into our reality with the infamous "Crash at Roswell" in 1947. Since that time thousands of people have come forward with their own experiences, including pilots, military personnel and whistle blowers, prompting thousands of books, published on every aspect of this amazing phenomenon.

Lorraine McAdam is one of those experiencers who has, since a child, been aware of other people who do not necessarily originate from this planet we call Earth.

Bravely they speak at UFO conferences and other platforms from all around the world. Talking from the heart, of night-time visitations, close encounters and abductions (military or off-world), marks and bruises on their bodies and even implants, several of which have been located in the body and medically removed. These people have to learn to adapt and live in two worlds, keeping silent at mealtimes when asked how their day went.

We still have some way to go to get to those who still refuse to believe and put things down to imagination, illusions or mistaken identity.

Read Lorraine's book and make up your own mind. A very kind and caring mother and professional teacher, who speaks from the heart when talking of her alien visitors. Even if you are already well acquainted with this type of experience, you will find much to ponder in Lorraine's book.

If you are a total skeptic, then perhaps it is time to open your mind and see the wonders that are happening around the world at this time, and historically· what has been happening for thousands of years.

We are facing great changes on this world at present and much more is waiting to change when we decide to open our minds and see.

Mike Oram, author of *Does It Rain in Other Dimensions?*

"There will be some readers perhaps—those willing to believe, or at least leave an open mind—that will no doubt ask, why her, why not me?" Lorraine tries to answer this question in her book.

A simple, truthful, riveting, intriguing, and sometimes frightening account of multiple encounters, experiences, with beings from other worlds, other dimensions...Who are these 'visitors'? What do they want? I gave some answers in my own books. Lorraine gives us some more insights here, and perhaps, some other important missing pieces of the puzzle...

Michel Zirger, author of *"We Are Here!" Visitors Without a Passport—Essays on Earth's Alien Presence*

Phantoms in the Night or ETs?

My lifelong experience of contact
with the paranormal

Phantoms in the Night or ETs?

My lifelong experience of contact with the paranormal

Lorraine McAdam

6TH
BOOKS

Winchester, UK
Washington, USA

JOHN HUNT PUBLISHING

First published by Sixth Books, 2023
Sixth Books is an imprint of John Hunt Publishing Ltd., No. 3 East St., Alresford,
Hampshire SO24 9EE, UK
office@jhpbooks.com
www.johnhuntpublishing.com
www.6th-books.com

For distributor details and how to order please visit the 'Ordering' section on our website.

Text copyright: Lorraine McAdam 2022

ISBN: 978 1 80341 305 1
978 1 80341 306 8 (ebook)
Library of Congress Control Number: 2022940300

A CIP catalogue record for this book is available from the British Library.

Design: Stuart Davies

UK: Printed and bound by CPI Group (UK) Ltd, Croydon, CR0 4YY
Printed in North America by CPI GPS partners

We operate a distinctive and ethical publishing philosophy in
all areas of our business, from our global network of authors to
production and worldwide distribution.

Contents

I would like to thank Michel Zirger for his kind advice and help with this book.
Michel is the author of *"We Are Here!" Visitors Without a Passport*.

For Chris, Adam and Mark, thanks for all your support.

For my dad, Keith, who always encourages me to give the best I can to everything I do.

For my mum, May, sadly deceased, who always stood by me through good times and bad.

Introduction

Writing this book has not been easy, and what I am about to relate will not be believed by the vast majority of people, which is why I have, albeit subconsciously, delayed its writing for so long. Indeed, only those in my close nuclear family know of any of the details of my story, which has been a lifelong one.

But in my heart I have realized that withholding my story — of what I have now come to believe is some form of ongoing extraterrestrial (ET) contact — is no longer an option.

In addition, the world seems to have moved into a more enlightened attitude towards those like me — call us abductees, experiencers, call us what you will — who have experienced and gone through this high strangeness that we loosely call 'contact.'

There will be some of you perhaps — those willing to believe, or at least leave an open mind — that will no doubt ask, why her, why not me? I have tried to answer this question in my book. I have my theories, having now widely read up on the subject, but I really have no definite answers as to why these things have happened to me. Besides, I would like to state categorically that, given the choice, I would not have asked for any of this to happen to me.

The fact is that the vast majority of us are not prepared or ready for contact! When it happened to me, it traumatized, frightened, puzzled, and confused me for a long time, because at first the possibility of ET contact was completely outside my closed Westernized Christian worldview. For years I was convinced that I was being attacked by demonic forces, particularly with reference to the 'Gray' aliens, whom I have seen frequently during abductions.

In contrast, all the benevolent contacts that I experienced in my interactions — with what I now realize were what we refer to

1

as the 'Nordic' aliens—I had put down to angelic interventions! I had been having these experiences since the mid 1970s, but it took me until the late 1990s to realize that there was much more to it than I had ever imagined. The book that first opened my eyes to the possibility of ET contact was *Communion* by Whitley Strieber, and I am eternally grateful to this brave writer for coming out about his own experiences at a time when, unlike now, the conditions for reception of such a book were definitely a lot more close-minded. However, for those like me who had experienced similar things, his book resonated, and I read it from cover to cover not once, but twice! Its contents disturbed me to such a degree that, for weeks afterwards, while mulling over its contents, I became subject to a form of post-traumatic stress disorder (PTSD). This probably happened because I was finally having to come to terms with what I had experienced for years. I was also obliged to visit my doctor for antidepressant treatment, blaming my depression and nervousness on stress at work.

Finally, once I had come to terms with the phenomenon, I went on a hungry search for any books that I could find on the subject.

Back then, in the early 1990s, you were obliged to look for the "alternative" or "esoteric/spiritual" section in local bookshops. There was no Google, no Internet; nothing at all like that existed. So, following my reading of *Communion*, I would frequently trawl through local and not-so-local bookshops on the hunt for more books on ETs and ET contact.

Obviously, as a result, my knowledge of the subject grew exponentially, and I realized—and this was comforting—that I was by no means alone!

However, I did not find the courage to share my experiences with anybody until well after the dawn of the millennium, when I contacted Mike Oram, whose book, *Does It Rain in Other Dimensions?*, really resonated with me, particularly with reference to benign contacts with the 'Nordic' aliens that I believe I too have experienced.

At the time I contacted Mike, I was going through a lot, and his kind reception of me helped me to understand some of the reasons why I might have experienced contact. We remain good friends to this day.

However, the fact remains that anyone who undergoes ET contact will experience the following, though not necessarily all of these effects, which I have experienced:

- You will most certainly be traumatized, both mentally and physically.
- You may become more intelligent than you were before contact started.
- You may become psychic.
- You may become more empathetic/intuitive.
- Your consciousness may be raised.
- Your religious beliefs will be challenged.
- You may become more spiritual and less religious.
- You may become more eco-conscious.
- You will be unable to believe your own eyes—that is, you will wonder if you are going mad or hallucinating.
- You may start to have frequent sightings of UFOs, in the sky, or on the ground.
- You may have sightings of human/non-human-shaped figures in your bedroom, in other rooms in your household, or in your place of work.
- You may have vivid dreams where you visit alien landscapes, or meet ETs face to face, and can afterwards recall everything clearly.
- You may undergo strange job interviews.
- You may experience the following:
  - poltergeist activity
  - sudden blackouts, which may be accompanied by a

buzzing noise around you, or a buzzing movement through your body, when late evening will move in a second to late morning
- ◦ ongoing depression
- ◦ post-traumatic stress disorder
- ◦ missing time that you can't account for
- ◦ unexplained strange marks and scars or burns to your skin
- ◦ unexplained rashes.
- Frequently, watches will stop or break.
- Light bulbs may explode in close proximity to you, or electronic equipment will malfunction around you, including airport security clearance equipment and electronic taps in bathrooms.
- You may acquire dark marks on clothing, particularly night clothing/bedding.
- Items of clothing may go missing and reappear later.
- You may find melted plastic coat hangers that have become welded together inside your closet.
- You may wake up outside your house, or in another room, for example the kitchen.
- Your family members, particularly your partner and parents, will not believe you and may ridicule you, or threaten to take you to see a psychiatrist, further adding to your trauma. (This is not necessarily because they are unsympathetic, but rather because it will be so far outside their experience that they will automatically move to a defensive position by laughing at you, assuming you are going mad or that you are hallucinating.)
- You will probably have a deep-seated, ongoing need to read up on everything you can in order to find out what has happened to you.
- You will want to make contact with other experiencers.

If you are presently experiencing suspected ET contact, then you have my empathy and sympathy. It is for you that I am writing about my own experiences, and while I realize that I will be ridiculed, possibly be the subject of debunking attempts, and get trolled for publishing this, I also know that there will be many out there who will understand what I have been through, and it is for you that I am writing my account. It is because of you that I have eventually found the courage to come out, as it were, and have done so at great personal cost to my marriage, to my career as a teacher, and to my reputation in general.

However, having undergone a number of spiritual promptings lately, I believe that I can no longer sit on the sidelines in the shadows and that it is time to share my story with the world.

Chapter 1

When I was a child, it seemed perfectly normal to converse with ghosts and invisible people

I never knew my grandmother on my mum's side, but I did know a relative of hers, an aunty of Mum's, who seemed to often predict the future of the local weather. She often used to stop talking mid-conversation, suddenly informing us that, "It will rain hard later on today." I didn't know whether to believe her or not, since the day would often be a dry one, but curiously, whenever this happened, it always did rain later on in the day. For this reason, behind her back, I called her Aunty Rain Hard.

Later on in my life, another spirit medium friend of mine would go on to confirm that I also had the gift of sight, or of being able to see the future—and also, that I had four spirit guides—and he told me that sometimes people would "take against me" for no other reason than that they were picking up on these four! This has sadly proved to be true, unfortunately, because in spite of being a considerate, caring, and extremely empathetic person, a lot of people have taken an immediate dislike to me during my life, for no reason that I have been able to fathom; and I have often been bullied by people, both at work and during time spent completing academic degrees.

Incidentally, there is a theory among empathetic people (of whom I believe I am one) that because we can easily unmask people—that is, read them like an open book—some people pick up on this, and they don't like you for it!

On top of this, I am also psychic. So, in addition, whenever I am in a room full of people, I can easily see who is truly happy, for instance, and who is pretending to put on a brave face; and I always know if someone is ill and hiding it, or indeed suffering silently in some other way.

Once, when I was attending a job club, I picked up that the job club leader—a man I incidentally got on well with—was a prominent Freemason, because I kept seeing him (psychically) in his Masonic robes; I knew about the Masons because I had read up on them. When I ventured to ask him if I was right, he was very impressed that I had picked up on this, and asked me to keep it to myself.

So, some people mind, and some people don't mind that I can read them, or to put it in a scientific way, I can read their *energy fields*; that is, if I want to of course. I am not saying that I go around willy-nilly, reading everyone's energy field like a regular psychic nosy parker! However, I do use this ability when I feel threatened by someone, or sense that they are hiding something from me. In addition, I always know when someone doesn't like me, no matter how hard they try to hide it.

If there is a ghost to be seen, I will often see it. For instance, during my years as a nurse, I was employed at a newly built nursing home that was built on the site of an old cotton mill, which had been demolished years before.

On my first day on duty—while administering medicines on the top floor, which was also the palliative care ward—I saw a little girl skipping up and down the corridor who looked as solid as you or me. The only odd thing about her was her dress; it was very old-fashioned, since she was wearing a long cream smock with pantaloons.

Assuming that someone's grandchild was visiting them, I went downstairs and mentioned it to the matron (head nurse). She gasped audibly, and looking shocked, she informed me that there were no visitors at the time I saw the child, as visiting didn't take place until the evening, and incidentally she would have had to let any visitors in through a door directly in front of her office. She told me that I had probably seen the resident ghost of a Victorian child mill-worker, and that I was not the only staff member to have seen this child; some of the night staff had also made a similar report.

No one at the nursing home had bothered to research the ghost, so we never found out who she was, but needless to say, from then on, I refused to work on the top floor on my own!

Aside from my propensity to see ghosts or spirits, of which this was not my first experience, there was also, according to my father, something very odd about the fact that a little girl of just 7 should persist in "talking to invisible people who appeared on the ceiling" (my own words).

Quite often, when I was a child—and I want to emphasize that this was a perfectly normal thing for me to do—I would concentrate on my blank bedroom ceiling, and suddenly it would begin to ripple and two men would appear to me. Now, these two were sitting behind what I would now describe as consoles, and wore identical navy-blue tops that had black turtlenecks. In the background, there were large windows behind them, and through these windows I could see tiny stars. So it would appear that these two were in space somewhere. Strangely, I didn't find this at all odd!

Moreover, I found that I could converse with these two, and they both seemed very friendly. They also looked like normal humans, though they were both very good-looking—one having short blond hair and the other having wavy dark hair—but that's all I can remember about them. I never even bothered to ask for their names, because it was as if there was no need to. Well, I would just tell them what I had been up to that day, and they would both smile and nod, and then fade out.

One day, my dad came into my room suddenly, on the pretext of asking me what I would like for supper, and he caught me conversing with them. His first reaction to this was to ask me: "Who were you just talking to?" For some reason, I didn't want him to know about my two 'friends,' so I just told him that I was talking to myself. This earned me a puzzled and concerned look from my father, and although he would still come into my room now and then without warning, he never asked me about them again. However, soon after my eighth birthday, those two men no longer put in an appearance, no matter how hard I tried to summon them.

Curiously, around the same time this stopped happening, during the summer of 1974, I had a very vivid dream that I had seen a cigar-shaped craft that had landed in a vast field. In my dream, I went into the middle of the field and stood close to this giant craft — when suddenly a man in a silver suit with shoulder-length blond hair came out of it, via a ramp that opened in its side. I ran to greet this man and he held me in his arms for a while, and to me it seemed as if I was just greeting an old friend.

Shortly after this, later in the year, I heard my mum conversing with my father, telling him that a huge cigar-shaped silver craft had been sighted in Wales.

I pestered my mother to let me see a picture of this craft in the newspaper, and it proved to look uncannily like the one I had seen in my dream! I stared at the photo for some time, and eventually I cut it out and put it in my scrapbook. For a long time after, I had the uncanny feeling that I had seen a craft like this many times before, but I just could not remember where.

Following these events, my grandmother suddenly died, and I could not stop crying for her to come back, as I had formed a really close bond with her.

One night, a few months later, she came to me in a dream and showed me that she was standing in a meadow filled with large white daisies. She told me that she was happy there and not to worry about her; then she took me to a small cottage and showed me that she was busy there, baking bread, just like she had in life. When I woke up from the dream I felt much better, and after that, I stopped crying, much to my mother's relief.

Nothing unusual happened for some time following this,

except that for some strange reason, in 1974, my mum decided to go on holiday without my dad, but instead took me and her father, who by that time was very old.

I liked my grandfather, Mum's dad. He always wore a flat cap, and he loved to smoke, which he frequently did, and no one had the heart to tell him that he was literally stinking the place up! We used to watch Laurel and Hardy repeats together on Saturday mornings, and we would both cry with laughter at their antics.

My mum and I often went to visit him in the nursing home that he lived in, and one fellow resident, appalled at his smoking habits, would repeat this catchphrase to my mum: "He's been smoking like a factory chimney, you know! He's going to set us all on fire one day, you watch, he will!"

This proved to be prophetic, as Granddad did indeed cause a fire in his bedroom. After that, to his chagrin, he was only allowed to smoke in the lounge of the home.

After he died, I would always know when he was visiting me because I would smell his favorite brand of cigarettes, Players, a British brand that he always liked. This would often happen during a period when I was living on my own in a little flat and was feeling a bit down or lonely, back in my early nursing days; and I have never smoked or allowed smoking in any home of mine!

Anyway, that year back in 1974, we had this little holiday together at a local seaside place, and during the holiday my mum broke the news to me that she and my dad had applied for a divorce. This really shocked me and I couldn't understand why it had happened; but I was going to have to get used to it, whether I liked it or not. By this time I was 11, and in the following September I was due to start at secondary school.

I was quite proud of my new navy-blue skirted uniform, and my pale-blue shirt and striped tie. My mum also bought me two secondhand dresses (the summer uniform) from another mother, as well as a blazer and a navy-blue raincoat for winter. So, my parents separated, and my dad bought a house close to my new school. Every night, I would walk down there and let myself in with a key, as sometimes he was on a late shift at the nearby factory where he worked.

My dad had no idea how to manage this old dilapidated house that was badly in need of an upgrade. I think for a time after the divorce, he went into shock over it; and it took him all of his energy just to carry on with life.

One night, shortly after my dad had moved into this house, a tall man with shoulder-length blond hair came and knocked on the front door, asking if I could fill up a plastic jug with water; this water was for his car, or so he said. I felt that this man's energy was different—not evil, or 'off,' just different. But I complied with his request and went to get him some water, wondering at the same time why he didn't just scoop some out of a nearby puddle. Whoever he was, he left an impression on me, and I can still see him, all these years later, standing on my father's doorstep, holding out the jug to me and dripping with rain. He had sloe-shaped eyes and a kindly face. Coincidentally, as I would discover later, so do the 'Nordic' aliens!

One day, when I was alone in Dad's house, I thought I saw a short little bald man standing at the top of the stairs. He was wearing old-fashioned striped pajamas. Feeling scared, I ran out of the house and knocked at the neighbor's house next door.

This lady knew my mum, and she tutted at me when I explained what had happened; but she let me stay with her until my dad came back. The neighbor told me that a butcher had lived in the house after his mother had died, and that he'd been on his own for a number of years and died there all alone. This story gave me the shivers, and I found myself feeling sorry for the stranger's ghost. I never saw him again, but I never felt comfortable in my dad's house following this, and I only went there when I knew Dad would be in.

Meanwhile, I went to live with my mum on a huge social housing development situated some miles away from my dad's home. But back then, people used to walk more, and being poor, I often walked all the way back to Mum's house from my dad's. This would involve walking through a nearby village, up a long wooded avenue, and through the huge housing estate where we lived: a journey on foot of at least four miles. In consequence, I must have been very fit without realizing it, and I became good at short-distance running at school—that and the long jump. Nobody could beat me, and I found that highly amusing, especially when the snooty middle-class kids couldn't beat me.

So life continued in a pretty mundane and normal fashion, until, that is, I arrived at the year 1976.

Chapter 2

Apparently, I am psychic and in need of an intelligence upgrade

My parents divorce

My experiences with what I now believe were both benevolent and not-so-benevolent ETs began in the summer of 1976. But first let me provide some background.

My parents had now split after an 11-year marriage that had dissolved into a less than acrimonious divorce. In fact, it had dissolved into a number of broken plates and hurled expletives, which I will not go into here.

Following this, I went to live with Mum on a social housing estate that had just been built. It was very big and stretched for miles from one end to the other. The houses were built with sandy-colored brick and must have been designed by a very bored architect, as they stretched out in row upon row of boxy, indifferent-looking terraces.

My mum and I were allocated a house on a close (cul-de-sac) at the northern end of this huge sprawling development. I remember her taking me to look around, and she was obliged to take a flashlight because autumn was coming in and it got dark quite early.

I was truly feeling heartbroken because of my parents' divorce, but at the same time, a part of me realized that their marriage had gone beyond fixing. So it was with a mixture of trepidation and excitement that I looked around our new end-terrace house on that late autumn evening.

My most vivid memory of that night is the smell of new wood and plaster that the house seemed to breathe out. There were three bedrooms in this terraced home (no 'bedroom tax' in those days). My mum allowed me to choose the largest one

13

for myself. Looking at it by the glow of my mother's flashlight, I grew excited about painting it to match my orange and white bedroom drawers, dressing table, and wardrobe — bright orange being a popular color back then.

We moved in two weeks later and there was plenty to do, unpacking boxes and taking delivery of a small green secondhand sofa and chairs, which were duly placed in the small dining room, along with a flower-patterned table and chairs, which were typical of the styles of that era.

We were to spend the majority of our time in this tiny dining/living room, which would prove to be boiling hot in summer and freezing cold in winter, unless I trailed two miles on foot in the snow to buy paraffin oil so that we could light the portable heater! A task I couldn't warm to, if you'll pardon the pun.

The fact was that my mother could not afford to use the expensive central heating systems put into these newly built 'boxes,' and would take to waving her arms about, and shouting like a demented banshee, if I so much as dared to switch on the heaters in any room. Consequently, I would wait until she was out and craftily warm up my bedroom, then switch it off and tuck myself under the covers. I would then have a good read of whatever books I had borrowed from the school library, or my *Jackie* teenage magazine, which came every week.

Alas, I did not get away with this for long, because when the electricity bill arrived, it sent my mother into a fit of apoplexy, and earned me an ear-bashing that I did not quickly forget. So off I went on my two-mile round trip for paraffin oil!

My mother would reserve the actual living room, a larger room at the back of the house, for any "posh visitors." She referred to this room as the "front room" and filled it with the elegant furniture kept from our previous house. These "posh visitors" turned out to be herself, her obnoxious boyfriend, and my uncle and aunt, whose affectations towards wealth and snobbery were something of a legend in the family, and of course, her close friends.

She would also insist that her then boyfriend, Anthony, should ensconce himself on the comfortable furniture in there. However, I was to keep out of this room at all costs (and I was never given sufficient explanation as to why).

Moreover, I was most put out when this boyfriend, who gave the impression of being a gentleman, later proved to be a philanderer and a cheat—having proved himself clearly unfit to grace any of Mum's lettuce-green velvet furniture with his cheating backside!

But she would always keep on seeing him. Needless to say, whenever he made my mother cry, which proved to be frequently, I would boil inside with a rage that would never quite go away, and this led to my playing frequent tricks on him whenever he deigned to call, such as placing whoopee cushions under the seat of the reclining chair that he always sat in. Gratifyingly, I caught him off guard a number of times with that one. I would also spit in cups of tea that I made for him, politely handing them to him while smiling wickedly.

Meanwhile, Margaret Thatcher had recently come to power, and my mum proceeded to curse her every time she put in a monochromed appearance on our cheap black-and-white television set. We couldn't afford color, and I didn't really care, as I preferred reading to watching TV.

The fact was, we were at the bottom of the social strata. My mum was a cleaner and a blue-collar worker, and because she was getting on in years, she chose to work part time. As a result, we were quite poor by the British standards of the time. In consequence, I got help with buying my school uniform and received free school dinners.

Back then, you had to hand in your conspicuous 'free' green-colored school dinner tickets while you were standing in the queue for lunch, and I was frequently bullied because of this by the wealthier kids at my comprehensive school. However, I did my best to ignore them, and sometimes I would kick them hard, earning myself a detention, while leaving satisfyingly large bruises on their neatly socked shins. I would sit in detention, quietly writing, "I must not attack my fellow students in the dinner queue," all the while vowing that I would better myself through education one day—a thing I would later succeed at, though this was still a long way in the future and would come with a little help from my 'friends.'

How to isolate your few friends and influence teachers: discover that you are psychometric!

One day at school, my friend Milly was sitting next to me at lunch, and I have no idea why but, on brushing against her, I suddenly got the most awful feeling that something was wrong at her home. Turning to her, and I still don't know why I did this, I asked if I could hold her watch for a moment. This got me an "Are you a nutcase?" look from her and others sitting at the lunch table. However, curiosity must have got the better of her, because she immediately took off her watch, a delicate old-fashioned-looking silver object, and the first thing I picked up was that it was not hers, but her grandma's. (She later admitted that she had lost her watch recently and had borrowed her grandma's.) I then went on to make the following alarming prediction.

My first prediction

"When you go home tonight, your grandma will have had an accident, but not a fatal one."

I was to regret imparting this negative information immediately it was out, as Milly was to prove in her immediate actions following my words. In short, she immediately stood up, leaving her half-eaten sponge pudding and custard, and screamed—rather too loudly—causing everyone around us to pause in their eating. She then proceeded with alacrity to quit the dining room, yelling from the back of it that if anything had happened to her grandma, she would hate me forever!

Being very embarrassed by now and feeling somewhat sorry for myself, but still clutching her watch, I immediately exited the dining room with the intention of chasing after her, only to collide with my grumpy maths teacher, Mr Corbert. This earned me a reproof for running, and a demand to know: "Just what the hell is going on here, young lady?"

Being really quite innocent in these matters at this juncture, and very new to my recently discovered psychic abilities, I immediately confessed to Mr Corbert, informing him that I was a psychic and could read objects. Expecting him to explode in a fit of rage, I watched him carefully for the telltale signs of his left eye twitching, or his face coloration changing from pale pink to purple. Luckily for me, none of these things happened, and Mr Corbert—a person I had previously written off as something of a narrow-minded, pompous, and cantankerous twerp—immediately asked me if I would read his watch for him following afternoon maths.

Later that day, I did just that, informing Mr Corbert that his wife would soon become pregnant with twin girls. I don't think I had ever seen Mr Corbert turn pale white, but he did that day.

A year later, my prophecy to him would come to pass, as I discovered on bumping into him in the corridor one day— whereupon he informed me that I had been correct and it had been discovered recently that his wife was indeed carrying twins.

"You wished that on me, didn't you!" he said, and marched off up the corridor in a fit of umbrage.

Meanwhile, my first prediction regarding Milly's unfortunate grandmother had also proved true, because, as it turned out, when Milly got home, her grandmother had been taken to hospital, having fallen down the stairs at lunchtime! Fortunately, she did make a full recovery.

A very strange series of experiences

The first of what I will call "strange experiences" that I had took place when I was alone in my bedroom at night. I was aged 12 when this first happened.

My mum was asleep in the bedroom next door, snoring like a buzz saw, and she did not wake up from that, ever!

The experience commenced as follows. The first time it happened, I became extremely scared, and to my utter mortification, I actually wet the bed and had to change all my bedding.

My body suddenly became completely paralyzed, and I began to vibrate from head to toe. In addition, an awful buzzing sound, like the sound of many bees, filled my head. Following this, I blacked out. I woke up in what felt like seconds but was, in reality, several hours later. It had seemed to go from nighttime to daylight, at least from my perspective, within a matter of seconds!

This was to happen *repeatedly*—at least once a week for the next two years, until I was 16.

There was never any warning, except that I would have strong feelings of foreboding, and I was unable to relax and fall asleep naturally as you should. Every time it happened, the daylight seemed to occur within seconds, rather as if I had been made to fall unconscious.

One night, I tried to fight back, as this had been happening for a number of weeks and I could sense a presence behind me when it did.

This particular night, 'someone' actually tried to wrap their arms around me, and I looked down, and dug my fingernails into what appeared to be a pair of very pale white hands with very long tapering fingers wrapped around my waist. At the same time, I sent this 'person' a telepathic message which contained a number of impolite expletives. Their response was to dig me in the back, which only served to earn them a further tirade from me, before I blacked out again.

When I woke up the next day, it was to discover black soot stains on the back of my pale-blue nightdress. Strangely, it was covered in them, and I remember staring at them and bursting into tears, thinking that my mother was probably going to have the hissy fit to beat all hissy fits when she saw this! She would then go on to accuse me of using a black crayon on my nightdress. In the event, this is exactly what she did, on discovering it in the wash basket later. Our conversation went something like this:

Mum: "Why have you put bloody black crayon all over your nightdress?"

Me: "For fun." (Did I mention that I was inclined to sarcasm?)

Mum: "Why are you so stupid? I'll be lucky to get that out. Do you think money grows on trees?"

Me: "Actually, I did. You mean to say it doesn't?"

Mum: "Don't you get clever with me, lady!"

So I tried the truth.

Me: "I have no idea how it got there."

Mum: "Well, you can just jolly well come here and give it a good scrub with the Fairy soap!"

Two hours later I had managed to get it all out. Needless to say, on staring into the blackened soapy water in the washing-up bowl, the totally bizarre nature of the whole situation suddenly hit me like a brick; and I found that I could fully understand my mum's refusal to believe me. Besides, I really had no answers for her anyway and was struggling to work out how those stains had got there myself.

Later that day, I also recall finding two of my black plastic coat hangers fused together in the wardrobe, and when I took them out, some melted black plastic rubbed off on my hand. To say I was shocked by this find would be an understatement, and I remember holding these coat hangers and examining them, feeling very frightened indeed. In the event, I threw them in the outside dustbin, because at the time, I just didn't want to think about what their presence implied. Looking back on this, years later, I still have to ask how two plastic coat hangers could become so hot inside my wardrobe that they actually fused to each other! I only wish that I had kept them to show to people, but I was so frightened by this event that I couldn't wait to throw them in the bin.

I can only draw the conclusion that I must be stronger mentally than I believe. I knew from Mum's reaction that no one would either understand or, indeed, believe me. So I carried on with my life as best I could. Simply put, I tried to just push it all to the back of my mind. But it was very hard to do this, and I often found myself crying uncontrollably, and very much alone with my fears around what on earth could be happening to me.

A week later: locked out

On another night, not long after what I have come to remember as 'black stain night,' while incidentally wearing this same nightdress—a long plain blue affair with absolutely no adornments to mention—I went through the usual strange scenario, but I have to presume that on this particular night, a mistake was made with my personage. Because I was to wake up in the back garden, with the back door firmly locked shut against me. How to explain it? This is how the ensuing conversation went with my mother, following my loud knocks on our back door, around 6 a.m.:

Me: "Let me in!"
Door finally opens after several loud raps of my fist upon it.
Mum: "What are you doing walking around in the garden in your bloody nighty at this time of the morning?"
Me: "I did it for fun!" (Please note aforementioned predilection for sarcasm.)

20

Mum: "Come inside this instant, you silly stupid girl!"

Me: "Mum, I swear that I don't know how I got out there. You saw yourself that the door was locked!"

Mum: "I suppose you climbed out of the window. I hope you haven't broken my downpipe!"

Me: (sarcastically) "Yes, of course I've broken it. You'll have to call the Council now and tell them that your wild daughter deliberately chose to visit the garden via her window, while balancing on the still miraculously intact downpipe, and then jumped off it at speed into some very prickly rose bushes, just for kicks. She went to all that trouble because she suddenly, and unaccountably, fancied a quick stroll around the garden, which of course you often do at 6 a.m.!"

Mum: "Don't you get clever with me, lady! I'll have you to the bloody psychiatrist if you keep carrying on like this!"

Me: "What's he going to do, give me a ladder?"

Mum: "Don't you get clever with me, lady!"

Alas, this high strangeness was to continue for years and I was never really believed, and I really do have to conclude that my poor mum sincerely thought that I was going a bit mad at the time. When I look back on these events, I really can't say now that I blame her, because who wouldn't leap to that conclusion?

I did, however, persevere in telling my mum over and over about these odd experiences; but she would always put it down to my having a vivid imagination, or being a touch hormonal, and consequently a tad mad!

Time after time, she would quickly dismiss my attempts, albeit clumsy ones, to articulate in words what was happening to me. She would write it off as 'time of the month' problems, and frequently threaten to take me to see a psychiatrist, although she never did carry out this threat.

When I look back now, I can understand her attitude because

let's face it: the whole thing was just baffling, and frankly, bloody terrifying all at the same time!

How to gain intelligence overnight: get abducted by aliens!

Now, this is the honest truth, and hard as it is for me to admit it, at the age of 11 I was a pretty average kid. I was absolutely awful at maths, and although my English wasn't bad, I failed to excel academically or stand out in any way at all from my fellows.

Consequently, on completing the 'eleven plus' exam, I was condemned to inhabit the middle-grade form at a local comprehensive school for the next five years.

Now let me emphasize here that the middle grade was not the top grade! Yes, let me admit to this here and now: I did not get anywhere near top grades (which were designated by the letters A and R, chosen for some reason that still baffles me to this day). No, I was instead allocated to the N form. Again, why this letter? To this day I have no idea, though my brother applied his own brand of logic to that one—saying, predictably, that the N obviously stood for *Numbskull!*

Anyway, there I was, feeling less than mediocre, and in awe of the As and the Rs, who subsequently proved to be quite good at boasting of their top-grade status and reminding you at every opportunity of their obvious superior intelligence.

And true to my N designation, I was (not to put too fine a point on it) hopeless at science, and also unable to recall any salient facts from history, biology, or geography, and just about able to scrape by in English lessons.

So there I was, merrily scraping through school subjects, averaging averages like a true average person—that is, until the strange blackouts and periods of missing time commenced.

Of course, in spite of this continuing high strangeness, I still led a reasonably mundane life in the interim. Then, shortly following my return to school after a long winter term and Christmas 1978, my yearly exams came around, and when they did, I swiftly proceeded to baffle both myself and all my teachers by coming top of the class in nearly every subject; and yes, even coming third from the top in maths! Because, suddenly and inexplicably, triangles and angles had started to make perfect sense; so had bacteria, map coordinates, and all things pertaining to the English language!

Alas, while this did not secure me an escape route from the infamous form group N for Numbskull, it did, however, win me several prizes at the less-than-exciting summer 'end of year' speech night, and a mention from the head teacher, who was probably as surprised as I was at my miraculous turnabout!

When my final year in school arrived, aged around 16, I had been mercifully given the chance to take exams in five GCE subjects, which I attained passes in, and this provided me with the requisite number of GCEs to become a trainee nurse.

What does "psychometric" mean?

In the sense that I use it here, I mean that this is a form of psychic ability whereby you can hold an object worn by, or carried by, a person, and pick up aspects of their past, present, and future merely by holding the object in your hand.

Is there reported evidence from other abductees of becoming more intelligent, being put back in the wrong place, having missing time, finding marks on clothing or their skin?

The answer to this question is a resounding "yes," and if you don't believe me, I challenge you to put this question into any good Internet search engine and do your own research.

Back in the 1970s, when these experiences first started happening to me, there was no such thing as the Internet or access to a search engine. So, I want to stress here that I made absolutely no connection at first with an ET presence.

At that time I was a Christian, and consequently I blamed all the activity on a demonic presence, and I prayed (a lot) and asked for help from my pastor! (See next chapter.)

Since that time I have read a great deal on the subject, commencing in the early 1990s with Whitley Strieber's iconic book *Communion*. This book opened my eyes to what may have happened to me and was also instrumental in guiding me to further books on the subject.

Today, of course, as technology has moved on, I have also done my own research on the World Wide Web, and I am in touch on Facebook with a number of other experiencers of both the paranormal and alien abduction.

Chapter 3

Two years later: I seek help from the Church and train to be a nurse

Being religious and a Christian at that time, and gaining absolutely no useful insights from my mother on what was happening to me, I decided, on reflection, to confide in some church friends. They surmised that I must surely be under attack from demonic forces and commenced to allot me a regular prayer slot, devoted solely to securing the eviction of said demons from my room.

In fact, one of my close friends—whose actions at the time I now think of as bordering on lunacy—actually took one look at a fine bone-china horseshoe that I had hung on my wall, and pointing to it, uttered the following words: "That's it, that is the door! That is what has let them in!" Following this ominous pronouncement, she grabbed the offending object and stamped on it with outraged abandon, shattering it into dozens of tiny shards that I would still be spearing my feet with weeks later! Now, that horseshoe had belonged to my Aunty Rain Hard, and my mum had to go and tell her that I had broken it, didn't she. But it was okay, because Aunty Rain Hard proceeded to inform me that Uncle had kept a perfect copy of it in the heavenly realms. Needless to say, I wisely kept silence about my friend's opinions regarding that particular 'Pagan' object.

However, at the time, I secretly hoped and believed that this might be the source of all my troubles. Alas, my friend's actions did no good at all, because things just proceeded to continue apace.

I want to emphasize here and now that I did not connect any of my experiences at this juncture with ETs, and chose to believe my church friends—becoming very scared indeed when prayers and shattered china horseshoes failed to secure the eviction of the interlopers in question.

However, the experiences continued, and would continue with fairly predictable regularity until I turned 16, when to my utter relief they suddenly stopped.

1982

Coincidentally, in the summer of 1982, two very odd Mormons called on me. I was in the house on my own when they visited, and they did their usual thing of talking about the Book of Mormon and their prophet.

However, what was a bit strange was that one of them, a tall blond Aryan-looking man with perfect skin and features (see drawing below), seemed to have what I can only describe as a strange energy. I didn't connect this at the time with the ET phenomenon, as I simply had never read about it or heard about it, but there was definitely something off with his energy.

I drew this as accurately as I could. I have a good memory for faces, and years later I can still remember this strange young man. His skin was slightly tanned, and perfect with no flaws to his complexion whatsoever. His eyes were a very pale blue and almond-shaped. His sweatshirt was navy blue, and so were his trousers. He came back to my house alone, a thing that is never done, as far as I have been able to ascertain via queries to the Mormon Church.

Because I feigned an interest in their work, telling them that any Christians were welcome to call, the blond man returned a second time, alone, a thing I later learned the Mormons don't do. I have a vague recall of him sitting next to me on our tiny sofa—the one allotted to commoners, not the posh lettuce-green one—studying me intently, while I, in return, was attempting to flirt with him, which he failed to respond to in any way at all. In essence, he appeared to be very much in control of his emotions, and refused any offers of drinks, including orange juice.

The strange thing is that I can't remember what we talked about at all, only that we sat and chatted. I have to wonder if he was the one controlling this situation. I didn't see him again for a long time, but when I did, years afterwards, he hadn't aged one bit! But more about this later...

I choose a career in nursing

In the same year that I met this man, I started a college course in pre-nursing skills, and a few times, when I went to catch my bus, there would be a beautiful blond girl waiting, all on her own, at the bus stop; and she too had perfect skin and features. (See my drawing.) In addition, her energy—which I picked up on, due to my psychic ability—felt different or odd. I actually found myself rudely staring at her, and she would persist in looking intently back at me, causing me to quickly look away.

The girl at the bus stop. Like the 'Mormon,' she too had a perfect flawless complexion, and long pale-blond hair. She had quite a pointed chin and larger-than-normal pale-blue eyes. She wore a plain navy-blue jumper, close tight-fitting leggings, and seamless black boots.

The funny thing about her appearances was that, because I lived on a council (social housing) estate, there would usually be at least a dozen people waiting for the early morning bus when I caught it, but whenever she put in an appearance, there was only her there and, obviously, me. I have to wonder now if she was one of what we now refer to as the 'Nordic' aliens—having only recently learned about them. I also ask the same thing of the Aryan-looking Mormon with the perfect skin.

Another strange thing, at least for me, was that I never managed to get into conversation with her, even though I felt drawn to her. Normally, I am one of those people who can, and will, initiate a conversation with anybody. I am that person who will talk to you on a train or if you are sitting next to me on a park bench! But, for some reason, I could not do this with this lady. In addition, her general demeanour was proud, and perhaps suggestive of a cold or indifferent disposition. I was only to encounter this young woman a handful of times, and she never appeared again after this.

Meanwhile, I completed my pre-nursing course and applied to a famous hospital in order to specialize in nursing people with learning disabilities and psychiatric problems. In 1984, I was accepted onto their nursing program and commenced my training.

In those days, nurse training was 'hands on,' and you did not undertake a four-year nursing degree as you do now. In essence, you spent eight weeks in nursing school, following this up with eight weeks on a specialized ward, and this ward would be specially chosen to coordinate with the theory work that you had completed in nursing school.

Nothing unusual happened to me during my first year.

However, at the beginning of my second year, there was a strange event while I was working alone on the night shift—yes, student nurses were left alone then. A lot has changed!

Let me explain. The hospital I worked in was a very grand Victorian affair with long sweeping corridors, attached to tall red-bricked houses which contained two hallways—an upper and a lower one—that led out onto two lots of wards. Each block was divided into sections designated by different letters, and each terraced building had a ground-floor and an upper-floor ward.

One night, I was about to go for my supper when an Irish nursing assistant from the ward next to mine, a lady named Geraldine, whom I had only met in passing up to this point, came running onto my ward, shouting for me to come to take a look out of the back kitchen window.

The two wards on each block shared a large kitchen. This particular kitchen had two floor-to-ceiling Victorian windows that you could open up, and they would literally afford you a panoramic view of the nearby fields.

It was close to harvest-time that night, and some of the hay had already been rolled into bales and placed in the field to which Geraldine now pointed.

Above this particular field, a bright orange ball hovered for some time, and both of us could hear and feel the humming noise coming from this object. I want to stress that this was not the setting sun, as that was close by, and in the process of setting, so this bright orange ball was separate from that.

We watched it together, until it just seemed to fade out. Well, Geraldine, being a very devout Catholic, immediately suggested to me that perhaps we had witnessed "a fiery angel." I wasn't at all sure what we had witnessed, and this was, incidentally, my first sighting of what are now commonly called UFOs.

We did report the sighting to the matron on duty, but she just mocked us both and said that it was probably the light from a tractor, refusing to take us seriously at all. And I have to say that this was a common reaction back then to any mention or suggestion of UFOs, or a sighting of their occupants. In addition, matrons back in the early 1980s were far more frightening and strict than they are today, and this one was no exception, and she went on to forbid both me and Geraldine to talk about the incident.

However, this did not stop us from discussing it on the bus

on the way home the next morning—Geraldine caught the same bus as me—as it traversed a number of villages on the way back to the town that I then lived in. One of these villages was hers, and we took the opportunity of travelling together to talk about this incident. We were both very angry at Matron's narrow-minded reaction to our story. However, attitudes back then to this sort of thing were far less open-minded than they are today; so in the end we both thought it best to let the matter drop.

Has there been a sea change in our attitudes to people who claim to have seen UFOs, or indeed claim to have been abducted by aliens?

I believe that the answer to this question is a firm "yes." Why do I say this? I believe this to be the case for a number of reasons, which I will go on to outline.

Today in 2022, most of us carry around mini-computers, known more commonly as smartphones. We did not dream of these in the early 1980s; all we had were dial phones, which even today have the power to render most millennials speechless! I once took my sons into a museum and asked them to engage in the novelty of dialing any number on one of them. Neither of my two sons could dial a full number!

Anyway, these smartphones have got instant access to things known as apps, and one of these is, of course, the camera app.

Now what happens when you give a camera to, well, an awful lot of people? According to smartphone statistics, "There are 5.11 billion unique mobile users worldwide in 2019, and 2.71 billion of them use a smartphone."[1]

That's a lot of people who are now able in an instant to point said phone at any peculiar object in the sky and simply click. As a result of this invention, UFOs have been captured both on film and in photos worldwide, and moreover shared and shared again on numerous websites, collectively known as social media—aka Facebook, YouTube and Instagram, to name a few.

This propensity to share photos and films, often clear images, taken by bystanders, has certainly made it more acceptable to claim that you have sighted a UFO, or strange phenomena in general, and this in spite of fakery and photoshopping.

Moreover, since the advent of social media, it could be argued that there has been a 'domino effect' in direct correlation with the number of people coming forward with their experiences—in that, if you see 'so-and-so' share their story on sites like Reddit, then surely you think: *I won't look like such a nut if I share my story on there too*, so someone, somewhere finds the courage to share their story of contact; and on and on it goes, until thousands of individuals are found to be sharing their stories.

Are all of these people deluded nutcases? I think not.

According to Nolsoe—as cited on https://yougov.co.uk site in 2021: "One in fourteen Britons (7%) even believe they've seen a UFO themselves. Men are more than twice as likely as women to believe so at 10% vs 4%."[2] That's a pretty high number of people in Britain alone who claim to have seen a UFO!

Moreover, there's been the invention of this little thing called the tablet or the Kindle, and this gives you instant access to any book with "alien," "ET," or "UFO" in the title more quickly than you can blink an eye! Hence, experiencers like me can download any number of testimonies, and books on the subject by researchers and theorists, and this need only be limited by your personal finances. Luckily, mine have been sufficient that I have collated a whole virtual library of information on this surprisingly wide-ranging subject!

What you will also discover, if you choose to dive down this particular 'rabbit hole,' is that this subject, in my personal opinion at least, has been deliberately kept secret for some time and deliberately ridiculed by the mainstream media since the 1950s—and I am by no means alone in this opinion, as you will discover, should you choose to research the subject yourself.

That has been the case up until recently, when I believe there has been a shift in consciousness towards those who profess interactions with the ET phenomenon; and this is because of all the reasons given above and more. So yes, there has finally been a definite shift in consciousness—and thank God for that!

And in case you are still doubting that there has been a definite shift in attitude towards UFOs and contact, go and take a look for yourself by simply typing in the words "UFOs and a shift in consciousness" into any good search engine.

Chapter 4

Summer 1986: A strange series of events occur while I am on a patients' holiday abroad

Nothing strange happened for some time after this one 'sighting' during my final training year, and I was left alone for a few years.

During this time, I qualified as a nurse, and went to work as a staff nurse in a community setting, looking after patients with learning, physical, and mental disabilities. As a result, I was asked to take some patients on holiday in the mid-1980s to a popular Mediterranean destination overseas.

I flew out with the patients and one other nurse, and we checked into our apartment.

That night, we went out to a restaurant to eat. Unfortunately, by the time we got back to the apartment, I had become violently ill and could not stop vomiting.

Surmising that I had been somehow poisoned with contaminated food, the nurse who was with me rang for an ambulance.

Meanwhile, I blacked out and came to in a hospital bed.

The strange thing was that, although I was very weak, I was embarrassed to find, on waking up in a hospital side ward, that there was a handsome blond Swedish-looking man in the bed next to mine! Moreover, he was surrounded by four equally pale-skinned, beautiful blond people, two women and two men, and I presumed they were visiting him.

On seeing me looking intently at them, one of the women (see my drawing below) came up to me and asked me how I was feeling, to which I replied that I was feeling extremely weak. I was also desperate to go to the toilet, and I asked her to find me a nurse to take me. Meanwhile, I was finding the energy coming off this whole group of people very odd indeed!

This is my drawing of the strange young woman who came to help me in the hospital when I was admitted with severe food poisoning.

She had high cheekbones and large pale-blue eyes. She also had pale blond hair and perfect flawless skin.

When the lady returned, she informed me that she couldn't find a nurse but had found me a wheelchair, and she would take me to the toilet herself, if that was okay. Strangely, I agreed to this, in spite of her being a complete stranger to me. Her energy felt very gentle, caring, and kind, but it also felt different. Again, having since read up on the subject, I am now mindful of the 'Nordic' aliens.

Also, why were there no actual nurses around to help, and why didn't I think to ring the buzzer next to my bed? The more I think back to this situation, knowing what I now know, I have to wonder about it.

After this incident, this young woman assisted me back to bed and I fell into a deep sleep. I woke up, and I could now see that it was dark outside.

Glancing at the bed next to mine, where the man had been, I noticed it was empty and neatly made up, and I surmised that he must have been discharged while I was asleep. I couldn't help wondering how he had managed to pack up and leave, though, without waking me—as obviously, when you leave hospital, of necessity you must at least tidy out your side locker, and surely this would have made some noise!

When the obviously Greek-looking night nurse, a woman,

came to give me some medicine and put a saline drip into my hand, I questioned her about the blond man in the bed next to mine.

Her reply shocked me—because she insisted that I had been in there *by myself* all the time, and that there had never been anyone in the bed next to mine, much less a blond man with four equally blond visitors in tow!

At the time, I did not associate this with aliens or any ET presence. In fact, due to my Christian beliefs, I actually put it down to angelic intervention, taking comfort from it and the fact that Jesus had taught us, via the Gospels, that strangers among us could be angels in disguise.

Puzzled by all this, but not scared, I asked the nurses repeatedly if I could attend the hospital chapel on the approaching Sunday; but they said I could only do that if they had a member of staff to spare to take me there, and I had to be satisfied with this.

When Sunday arrived, another very Greek-looking nurse, who told me her name was Carolla (see my drawing below), came to assist me with my morning ablutions, and she asked me if I would like her to take me to the chapel that day. Because I was anxious to say prayers there, I was happy to agree, even though there would not be a service on—a strange thing in and of itself in a Catholic country on a Sunday!

She quickly obtained a wheelchair and helped me into it, and then she took me via the French windows that led off the ward to the hospital gardens, down a deserted path where cactuses were in bloom, to a very small white chapel building.

The funny thing about this 'chapel' was that it was extremely dark inside on entering it! In fact, I could barely see my hand in front of my face! Nonetheless, because Carolla's presence was so reassuring, I allowed her to take me in there anyway. The next thing that happened seems very strange when I review it now, but at the time, it was as if I was numb to any fear.

Carolla suddenly said: "Come and talk with one of our elders. He will help you to feel better."

I was feeling so sad and down that I was happy to agree to this; so I let her put me in a pew and this 'elder' was suddenly there next to me! The funny thing was, as I look back now, I have no memory of his face. In fact, the darkness in there shrouded his face, and I can only remember his deep strong voice and his words to me. I also have no memory of him walking up the aisle, or of him coming from behind me to sit next to me. It was as if he was just suddenly there next to me, as if he materialized out of thin air! Moreover, why on earth did she refer to him as an "elder" in a Catholic country, and not as "the father," or "the priest"?

I have remembered his words for all of my life. Our conversation went like this:

Elder: "Why did you want to come to church so much?"
Me: "Because I wanted to pray and feel God's presence."
Elder: "But you didn't need to come to a church to find God. God is everywhere! He is all around us!"
Me: "Is he? How can that be?"
Elder: "Yes, God is all around us, and one day you will understand this."

I don't remember any more of this conversation, and at the time, I saw this as a perfectly normal visit to a very dark chapel. It only struck me the next day that something strange had occurred!

His prophecy, that one day I would understand, has now come true—as I no longer confine my beliefs to the narrow framework taught by Christianity, but have expanded my beliefs. I am now more of a pantheist, and do indeed believe that God is in everything, including us, and that everything is a reflection of a central creative consciousness, or force, that I refer to as "source."

But I digress.

The following day, a new male nurse came to help me with my morning shower, and I asked if it was Carolla's day off. The nurse gave me a puzzled look and informed me in no uncertain terms that there was no nurse named Carolla working on this ward! I was quite shocked by this, as I had been planning to ask Carolla for her name and address so that I could keep in touch with her after I was discharged. I had really warmed to her because she had been so kind to me. So I actually began at this point to wonder if I was going completely mad!

Moreover, shortly after this exchange, the senior doctor put me on antipsychotic medicine, probably due to the fact that I kept going on about all of these non-existent people! But I swear that I did not hallucinate or dream any of these people up!

The mysterious nurse Carolla, who turned out not to exist.

On returning to the UK, my life carried on pretty much as normal. I transferred to nursing on a therapy unit and started working daily hours instead of shifts. I also decided to move in with a friend of mine to save money on bills.

As I have stated earlier in the chapter, at the time of these events I tried to interpret them through the filter of Westernized Christianity. That is, I looked upon the persons that I encountered as angels, or helpers, at a time when I had been extremely ill with food poisoning in a foreign country.

However, looking back now, I am more convinced than ever that these people—or what I suspect now were ETs—while indeed coming to my assistance, were also, in the process, for whatever reason, attempting to expand my consciousness beyond the narrow confines of my core beliefs. But the question that begs to be asked is, why me? Why the ongoing contact that continues even today? What was it about me that attracted them? Why was I worth their trouble? Why am I still worth their trouble?

I have my theories as to the answer to these questions, and I am sure that they will correlate with those of other experiencers. I have since found out from research that many experiencers are contacted for the reasons outlined below (not that this is a conclusive list).

1. I have evidence of a Rhesus-negative blood line

Some of my family members have the rare Rhesus-negative blood type. What is the significance of this? It has been theorized that those who are Rhesus-negative may have alien DNA—yes, you read that correctly, I did say that!

If you doubt me here, and I can understand that people will, please go and put the following inquiry into any good search engine: "What's special about Rhesus-negative blood?"

2. Am I awake?

What do I mean by "awake"? I suppose this will be interpreted differently from individual to individual. However, my definition is not going to be a mockery of present-day extreme left-wing politics—no, I want to stress here and now that I am not about to declare myself part of some 'woke' community.

My own beliefs about being awake are quite different from this. To explain, I will have to go back to when I was just a child.

The fact is that I never quite felt like I ever fitted in well on this planet—and maybe because of certain psychic abilities, many will see me as being odd anyway.

The morals of this planet's leaders, and the ways they conduct their affairs, have always seemed to me to resemble—if you will pardon me for saying so—something akin to a bunch of lunatics running their own asylum. A bit of a cliché, I know, but I won't be the first to say this about world politics or the conduct of politicians.

In despair, I turned to Christianity for answers at a very young age, having read the four Gospels by the age of 12, and having committed my life to Jesus and undergone full-immersion water baptism shortly after. I often prayed long and hard on my knees for the world at that tender age, seeing a lot that was awfully and horribly wrong with it.

Moreover, my history lessons at school only served to reinforce my already dim view of Earth's leaders by allowing me to become fully informed about the horrors of the First and Second World Wars, when I learned of the wholesale slaughter of a generation of fit young men, and about the atrocities committed on the Jews in German concentration camps. I also learned about the Japanese refusal to surrender to the Allied forces, and the eventual dropping of the first atom bomb on Hiroshima. What a horror show that all proved to be!

In addition, I would watch the news on TV, and despair at the plethora of bad news, seemingly deliberately churned out on a daily basis. My mother was addicted to the news broadcasts, and she also read newspapers on a daily basis, so there was no shortage of world news and horrific headlines in our house.

I was appalled at the way that politicians and leaders seemed to persist in creating further wars; and I watched as terrorists bombed innocent civilians without consequence or thought, and how sides were taken for the gain of things like a monopoly on oil, or mining rights, or often for mere religious/cultural or racial affiliations and reasons.

Observing all this, I often felt like a visitor from another planet, and that I had come from somewhere far more advanced than this troubled earth—where I was clearly living through a dark age!

It didn't take me long to work out that he/she who owns everything here has the power to manipulate all of the issues mentioned above, and so shift global opinion in whatever direction they so choose.

So was I awake? Was this unusual for a 12-year-old? My mother thought it was, and she frequently told me that I was getting too caught up with world events and that I was getting depressed as a result. Could you blame me? I was poor and I knew it; therefore I felt essentially powerless and that my opinion didn't matter. But apparently it did matter, because, like thousands of others I was yet to meet, I was indeed very much awake, and far more powerful by dint of being human than I was yet to realize!

What do I mean by this? Well, if one person thinks that something is badly wrong, maybe they are in a minority, but if thousands of people, or even millions of people, start to think like this, does a shift in consciousness take place? If enough of us object to something, does change happen?

I personally believe that it does, because I have seen shifts towards a better humanity happen in my own lifetime.

In just 30 years, there has been a greater movement towards racial equality and sexual equality, and a move away from obvious bigotry towards religion, ethnicity, and culture.

There has also been a movement away from religion towards spirituality, and to caring for the environment and creation in all its forms.

This has not happened in a vacuum; it has happened because people have made it happen, and moreover, they have cared passionately enough to create change. So don't tell me that humanity cannot change. The truth is that often, those who suffer humiliation, deprivation, oppression, and bigotry at the hands of others are the ones most in a position to change and challenge it! This is as true now, with the illegal impositions caused by the advent of Covid-19, and the consequent impact on our individual freedoms, as it has ever been. If enough people object and challenge, change will become, I believe, inevitable.

So did 'they' choose me for these reasons? The answer is that I don't know, but since making contact with other experiencers online, I do know that there does seem to be a correlation between being "awake" as I define it here, and being an experiencer of ET contact.

3. Are they searching for family?

This partly relates to my other point above about Rhesus-negative blood. However, I also have to consider that the Earth, as it stands, has been here for many thousands, if not millions, of years. I will not be the first or last person to consider that there is a possibility that there have been higher civilizations, equivalent to our own in knowledge, that existed prior to ours.

I don't want to enter into controversy here, but the truth is that there is a plethora of knowledge out there now to suggest that we are not the first to reach a high state of civilization. There are also numerous authors who have conducted research on this subject, pointing to the evidence of early writings taken from the Sumerian and Greek philosophers and writers, not to mention the irretrievable loss of the library of Alexandria.

There is also, I believe, sufficient evidence of a worldwide flood that took place some 10,000 years ago, tracked through the myths of most nations on Earth, and this should warrant our attention, if only to make us marvel at the similarities between the stories of nations as wide apart as New Zealand, Iraq, Ireland, and India! And, moreover, in their pre-civilizations' writings, we can find evidence of flying craft, atomic bombs, and the humble battery, not to mention amazing architecture and archaeological finds that show an obvious knowledge of very advanced mathematics. Go do an engine search for yourself and find out more about this; please don't just take my word on any of this.

So, in light of these great flood myths, I would like to pose the question: Could some of our ancestors have got off the planet to form a breakaway civilization elsewhere? That being the case, could some of our distant relatives be coming to Earth to effectively find their own families via DNA testing? Are they looking for their own? This would be one reason at least to initiate contact, and ETs that look very human have been documented. In fact, there are those that look so human that, frighteningly, at least to some, they can pass themselves off among us without detection. If you don't believe me, just put the phrase "Human-looking ETs" into any good search engine.

4. Am I descended from ETs?

The other intriguing possibility I would like to put forward relates closely to the previous one, and that is that human-looking ET races may, thousands of years ago, have settled here from other planets, eventually mating with Earth humans and contributing their DNA to ours.

Is there evidence for this? The answer is: yes, there is, and I suggest that you look at the ancient Sumerian civilization first if you want to research this further; also you could try putting the phrase "Annunaki ETs" into any good search engine.

I would also recommend the following illuminating books/ authors:

- *Escaping From Eden* by Paul Wallis
- *The Missing Lands* by Freddy Silva
- *Slave Species of the Gods* by Michael Tellinger

So, is this why I drew their interest because, via my DNA, they found out that I am related to them? The answer is that I have absolutely no idea; nor, I suspect, would a look at my DNA get me any closer to an answer, because, if they are enough like us as to be indistinguishable, where do you start?

5. Am I a 'Volunteer Incarnate'?

This is going to sound odd, even far-fetched, but stay with me, because if you believe in the possibility of reincarnation, we are about to make a leap of imagination.

What if I'm not from here? By me, I don't mean my body, which is obviously from Earth, but what we refer to as the "soul" or "spirit"; sometimes this is also called the "essence."

As I've said previously, I have, since being a child, felt uncannily like I don't really belong here. I then add my suspected ET contact experiences in, and I ask if, being more advanced than us in every way, spiritually as well as technologically, do some ETs know who has volunteered from among their own? Do they have a way of knowing?

For those of you who doubt the possibility of reincarnation, go and google the stories of the experiences of those thousands of children documented by Professor Ian Stevenson (see book below). I would ask you to read about this with an open mind, before cynically dismissing reincarnation as a strong possibility.

In addition, I will add one final comment: If people reincarnate over and over again on Earth, why not people who are not from Earth?

For further reading on this, I would recommend:

- *Coming Back* by Raymond A. Moody MD
- *Where Reincarnation and Biology Intersect* by Ian Stevenson MD
- *Return to Life* by Jim B. Tucker MD
- *The Three Waves of Volunteers and the New Earth* by Dolores Cannon

Chapter 5

I become an undergraduate, go through marriage/divorce, and undertake a very strange job interview

After nursing for a number of years, I felt that I wanted to return to university to complete an English degree in order to teach, so I moved to my friend's house, two towns away, and carried on part-time nursing there, working two nights per week in a nursing home for geriatrics.

As I wanted to study for a degree, I was admitted to the mature student's pre-degree course at a certain town's now well-established university. I managed to get through this, and became a mature undergraduate at the age of 28.

I continued to live at my friend's house, and she introduced me to the young woman next door, who was called Mandy, and we became very close friends.

1992

It is worth mentioning that when I moved in to live temporarily with another friend during my final undergraduate year, the same 'abduction' scenario took place there that had occurred in my teens, and it was very frightening.

However, I can only recall one time that this happened, and it was just after I had moved in with this new friend. Again, I was paralyzed, and I remember that I also felt a very cold icy hand touch mine, before I blacked out in bed, coming to much later in the day. I moved out of her house two months later, after unwisely marrying my current boyfriend.

1990s: Marriage/divorce and a very strange job interview

At the start of the 1990s, I unwisely got married to a man I had only been seeing for six months. When we first married, we rented a small house.

Several odd things happened to me while I lived at this rented house.

The first thing was that, after not living there very long, I went outside to get some air as it was summertime, and I had been revising for hours for my final-year exams and needed a break. So I took a kitchen chair into the small back garden, made myself a cup of tea, and had some time out.

I was just sitting looking up at the empty blue sky, when suddenly, a red-colored 'object' zoomed into view and came to a sudden stop right above me. I stared at this round object for some time. I even went to get my then husband to ask him what he thought of it, so he witnessed it too. He said it must be some kind of plane, but I ridiculed this, pointing out that a plane wasn't cylindrical in shape, and could not just stay still like that for so long. I was vindicated in this when it suddenly shot off into the distance at great speed! I have no idea to this day what this thing was.

Moreover, after that happened, some very odd and frightening things started to occur. For a start, I started having vivid dreams during the night. During these dreams, I found myself talking to a man with brown hair, who wore overalls that were pale brown—what looked like a mechanic's overalls. I can't remember what we talked about. I always woke up from these dreams feeling very frightened, and I started to find stains on my night clothes, often black smudges similar to the ones I had experienced previously (see earlier chapter), that had not been there when I went to bed, as I always wore clean night attire. I also found unexplained bruises on my thighs and upper arms. People will ask me why I didn't photograph evidence of this; the only explanation or excuse that I can give is that I was so unnerved by it that I just wanted it to go away, and taking photos would only make it seem more real and confirm it as

45

part of my ongoing reality.

While we lived there, I applied for a part-time job in a large city, in sales. I saw the advert in the local paper, or thought I did, but this job interview proved to be very strange indeed.

For a start, while I can remember getting off the train at the city's station, I have no recall of how I arrived at the offices where the interview took place. Surely, even years later, you would recall a street or road?

Moreover, when I arrived I was greeted by a young blond-haired, pale-skinned woman. (In retrospect, I ask myself now, was she a 'Nordic'?) She also had energy that felt strange to me.

All I can remember is that the 'office' walls were yellow, but totally blank, with a total absence of pictures, notices, or calendars! When have you ever come across an office with nothing on its walls? I asked if they had just moved into the building, but the woman failed to reply, and just smiled at me and asked me to wait. There were some red plastic chairs, so I sat on one of these, while she sat behind a bare wooden desk. Oddly, there was nothing on this desk—no typewriter, no papers, no telephone. This struck me as strange, even at the time.

The office door was slightly ajar, and as I sat facing it, I noticed that cars were constantly going past below. Oddly, these cars were all sky blue in color and contained handsome blond male drivers! Were they Nordic aliens?

Eventually, I became desperate for the bathroom and asked this woman where it was. She reacted by becoming all flustered, and said that there was no bathroom available for interviewees. I then asked if I could use the staff toilet, and she got even more flustered, and replied that I was not allowed! Now, I ask you, what recruiting office would be without an available toilet?

At length, a tall man, this time looking very earthly, and of

African racial extraction, came out of a side door and welcomed me into another very blank white office. His accent was British, but with no discernible dialect; the young woman's accent was also perfect British, but robotic.

He sat down behind an equally empty bare desk.

Expecting him to ask me about the job, I sat down opposite him and waited, but instead he started asking me questions about my ability to read objects! For a start, how did he know I was psychometric? I never readily offered this information to him. Then he removed his wristwatch and asked me to read it. Oddly, I didn't mind doing this. The strangeness of the whole situation only started to scare me afterwards, but oddly I felt very calm while it was happening. I could not read his watch at all. Usually I pick up a lot of things from an object that someone constantly wears, but I just could not read this watch; and I handed it back to him and told him this.

He seemed very pleased about this and placed it back on his wrist. He then told me that all the sales jobs had gone and apologized for bringing me to the city. Then he showed me down some steps at the side of this building, and conveniently, he placed me in a waiting city cab at the bottom of these steps.

I looked in vain for a street name, but could not see one; the building outside appeared like a plain set of white boxy-looking buildings, one on top of another.

Now, mobile phones didn't exist then, and there were no phones on either his or the receptionist's desks. So how precisely had this taxi driver, who incidentally knew to drop me off at the correct station, got called without my asking him? (He looked perfectly ordinary, in case you were wondering.)

I returned home and tried to forget about this strange experience, but it kept nagging at my subconscious and I found myself having dreams about it.

But before I go on...

Is there evidence of any other people experiencing strange job interviews similar to the one I experienced, as related above?

The surprising answer is "yes," according to the authors Carol Rainey and the late Budd Hopkins. If you want to find out more about this, I would recommend that you read their book, *Sight Unseen*, where three young women are mysteriously summoned to interviews in office settings. I have read this book myself and the women's experiences closely mirror my own.

I get married and divorced in short order

Life carried on pretty much as normal after that. I got married in the autumn of that year, but my marriage was not destined to last. The truth was that following our wedding, my husband began to show what I now believe were his true colors—often becoming abusive towards me.

I was trying desperately to get through the final year of my degree, and the last thing I needed was to be homeless! So for some time, at least a year in fact, I endured my husband's bad behavior and finally graduated; but there was trouble ahead for me.

Christmas of that year came and went, and I often found myself making excuses not to go home, frequently sleeping at the house of a kind friend I had made through the Church. I had met her at Sunday services, and I had plucked up the courage to share with her what was happening to me at home. Of course, she advised me to leave him immediately, but I wasn't ready to give up on my marriage yet.

Things came to a head, though, in the following year, when on returning from work, I accidentally allowed a pan of curry to boil over, and my husband, on seeing the dried-up mess, attacked me verbally and physically. I finally conceded that I would have to leave him.

Resolving to do so the next day, I rang my friend, who offered me temporary accommodation while I searched for somewhere else to live. She also helped me to find a lawyer, and I was able to apply for the legal aid to begin divorce proceedings on the grounds of unreasonable behavior.

I will make no bones about it—this was a very difficult time in my life. My husband's treatment of me had totally taken away any confidence I had, and although I badly wanted to undertake a Master's degree, which I incidentally had been accepted for, I ended up, to my utter regret, having to defer a place that I was never in the end to take up.

My friend could not let me stay with her for long, as she had several children to take care of, and moreover, her house was very small and already cramped with her husband and little ones. So I asked a relative if I could move in with him, and reluctantly he offered to put me up for a few weeks until I could find something.

I had very little in the way of savings at that time, and struggled to find a full-time nursing post, but I was obliged to put any aspirations towards teaching on hold and return to nursing in order to earn money and survive through this period.

Finally, I managed to secure a staff nurse post at a private nursing home with palliative care facilities. The only drawback to this was that it was a night position, but beggars could not be choosers.

I took up the post, working four 12-hour night shifts per week.

Meanwhile, the Council had provided me with a ground-floor flat on a small social housing development, and I had obtained some secondhand furniture, a bed, and some secondhand electrical items that my parents helped me to acquire. At first, the flat was quiet, and I made friends with the lady above me, but my luck was about to run out again!

Chapter 6

Noisy neighbors, a healing visit to a psychic shop, suspicious males, and a strange series of events

I had only been in this flat for two months when the woman above me moved out and two young men moved in to replace her, and they turned out to be terrible neighbors. Although they knew I was a nurse, working nights, and although I asked them not to play loud music during the day, they completely ignored me, and carried on playing loud booming music at all times of the day and night. I was actually glad to get away to work!

During this time, my divorce papers came through and I immediately reverted to my maiden name. However, the noise above me was driving me around the bend, and in despair one night, I rang my mum, holding the phone out for her to hear it. Thankfully, she told me to hand in my notice on the flat immediately, and come and live back with her until I could find something else.

So, for the third time that year, I packed up my meagre belongings, gave away all my furniture to a charity, and moved back in with my mum, who offered me a tiny little bedroom at the back of the small terraced house where she lived at that time, having moved away some years ago from the equally boxy terrace on the large housing estate described in earlier chapters.

Nothing untoward happened while I was experiencing all of this mental angst, but I started to experience very bad depression, no doubt due to what I had been through in the months that had passed. My doctor put me on a temporary dose of antidepressants, and I was given inhalers for newly diagnosed asthma problems.

A revelation occurs when I read a very strange book

While out shopping one day, I came across *Communion* by Whitley Strieber.

At the time, I was still working on nights. Well, I started reading *Communion* on my night shifts, and no one seemed to bat an eyelid at the book's strange cover, or judge me.

I was frankly shocked and frightened by the face on the cover of this book, as I had seen faces like it before; it was the face of the typical 'Gray' aliens, or what are known as the 'Zetas,' and it stared out at me from the cover, causing me to undergo flashbacks of that same alien face from years ago when the 'experiences' had first started. I now recalled what, at the time, I had thought to be a vivid dream. In this dream, two strange white creatures with very large eyes, and thin elongated fingers, had floated me out of bed and through my bedroom wall. I actually recall seeing spider's webs in the wall and the outer casing of plaster board as I passed through it to the outside of my bedroom, eventually emerging outside, floating just above my bedroom window. When I looked up, a large cylindrical craft was hovering above me, and I was floating up towards an electric-blue light on the underside of this craft. So, you will understand that this book by Whitley Strieber seemed to me to be a revelation, and a confirmation that I, ordinary average me, a then 28-year-old staff nurse, was being contacted by what I could only now conclude was an ET presence. But up until reading it, I had never considered this as any kind of possibility—because, being a Christian at that time, I had put all these experiences down to some kind of demonic persecution of me and had prayed a lot for it to all go away, which of course it didn't.

To put it succinctly, the book helped me to put two and two together and start to make four.

Moreover, on my first night in my new job, I had a paranormal encounter with the ghost of a dead girl, dressed in Victorian dress (see earlier chapters), only to learn later that that ghost had been seen by other staff, and that the site on which the home was built had once housed a cotton mill of the sort that were very common during the Industrial Revolution in the United Kingdom.

I couldn't keep this sighting to myself, and the staff under my authority quickly assumed, rightly, that I was psychic. This actually endeared them more to me, as I was happy to read rings and watches for them during coffee breaks, using my psychometric abilities, picking up on what usually proved to be accurate information.

At that time, a former close friend of mine came back into my life. I had previously known him through the Church, and he had been a friend years before, but we had lost touch.

One day, I was walking back to my flat—I had not yet moved—and there he was, sticking his head out of his car window and shouting for me.

After that, we got back together as friends, and he took me all over the place dancing, which proved to be great fun, as he would teach me the lady's dance-steps to all kinds of dances. I really enjoyed dancing and remember this period of my life with fondness.

One day, knowing about my gift, he took me to visit a psychic shop. I was just weighing a crystal ball in my hands, when I caught the shop's owner hovering behind me.

"You have psychometric abilities?" he said, in a rhetorical manner.

I nodded and bought the ball. The next thing was that he asked me if I would like to come and be the psychic reader for a day at the shop, and said that he would pay me for my time.

I agreed to do one session only, and my friend agreed to bring me, as I didn't drive back then.

However, during the next few weeks, before I was due to do this session at the shop, the events happened that I have related above—having to leave my flat due to noise nuisance—and I was obliged to move in with my mother to escape.

This left me very down and under the weather, and when I eventually arrived at the shop, the shop's owner (I can't recall his name) somehow just knew that I was in need of healing. Forbidding me to do the morning session, he somehow got a young man, whose name I cannot recall either, to treat me with crystals at very short notice!

I was a bit skeptical about this, though the healing power of crystals has now been documented. This young man asked me to lie down, and he then placed some crystals on various parts of my body. I did feel a lot better when he had finished. I have no idea, even to this day, how these healing crystals work on the body; though I now have an understanding that they rebalance the body's chakras.

When I went downstairs, the owner of the shop remarked that I looked much better. He paid the young man, and he also said something to him—and to this day I have no idea what he meant; he said: "Thanks for helping her. She's one of us."

Now, this could merely have meant that I was a fellow psychic, though young and inexperienced as yet with my abilities.

I have wondered, though, in light of my other experiences, and of what I now know years later with regard to the 'Nordic' ETs, if he meant one of two possibilities.

Firstly, that I was part of a soul family of incarnates that are, frankly, not from Earth.

(For more about this I would recommend that you read *Awakenings* by Mary Rodwell and *The Three Waves of Volunteers and the New Earth* by Delores Cannon.)

Or, secondly, that he and possibly the young man, who was blond and blue-eyed, could be ETs incognito, as there is evidence to suggest that some of them blend in with us perfectly well, and you would be hard put to tell them apart from us—or so I am now informed; and that he recognized something in me, relating either to genetics or spirit/soul, that I was not at that time aware of.

(For more about ETs walking among us, I would recommend that you read *"We Are Here!"* by Michel Zirger.)

Needless to say, this experience has haunted me for years. I never did return to the shop — except that recently I did go back, and it was still there, but it was closed. I made this visit in 2021, 26 years after I had last visited!

Two suspect strangers cross my path

One night on the way to work, in summer 1993, I met a colleague of mine, Mike, a nursing assistant, on the bus that took us to work. We got on well together, and we talked and laughed all the way to our stop, until we got off and walked up the road towards the hospice.

Suddenly, we were stopped by two handsome men in shirts and chinos, and they asked us for directions to the bus station.

I know this is going to sound odd, but I will swear that one of them was the same handsome blond pale-skinned Aryan-looking Mormon I had met back in the 1980s! (See my drawing in Chapter 3.) I couldn't help staring at him for this reason, as he hadn't aged one bit! His colleague, also handsome with perfect skin, had a darker, olive skin tone and dark brown hair.

My colleague teased me afterwards and said that I obviously found the blond one attractive, but he totally misunderstood what was going on inside me — whilst I was staring at him, it felt as if we connected in some way, as if he was indeed saying: *"Yes, it is me!"*

High strangeness at work

Things were to take an even stranger turn at work that night, when at around 1 a.m. a patient's buzzer went off on the top-floor ward. This was unusual, as dementia patients seldom rang their buzzers. However, since a check was due, I volunteered to go.

Before I go any further in relating this incident, I will state that there were *eight* staff members on shift with me that night, and that *at the very least, they witnessed my being missing for over an hour*. I mention this because I believe it is significant in proving the credibility of my story.

This is what happened from my perspective: August 1993

At 1 a.m.—I remember the time, because I was always in the habit of looking at my fob watch, as nursing reports must state times of incidents, and I was mindful that the buzzer's going off might foreshadow a medical emergency since residents often had TIAs (minor strokes)—I went up to the top floor, taking the lift, as it was quicker.

I immediately felt scared on exiting the lift, for no reason that I could fathom, other than that the top floor corridor had a very strange atmosphere. I was obliged to walk around a corner to reach the room where the buzzer was going off, and could not at first see around that corner—until I traversed it.

On coming around the corner, I was shocked to see two strange figures standing at the bottom of the corridor, adjacent to the room from whence the noise came; moreover, the buzzer stopped as soon as I saw them.

I will attempt to describe these two: they were definitely not human, having large pointed ears, large noses, no hair that I could see, and a leathery-looking skin, which appeared to be a dull brown colour. I read them as being a female and a male.

The male was taller (see my drawing below), and I noticed that the female wore a headscarf wrapped around her head, much in the style of women from India—I failed to see much of the male in detail, except for his large pointy ears and his greater height; he was at least 7 feet tall—and added to this, they both had blood-red eyes.

Feeling absolutely terrified, I then ran for it; and hid in a nearby bathroom, having the self-preservation to pull the buzzer for help.

Another staff nurse on duty with me, a woman called May (I don't remember her surname), then appeared, after what felt like ten minutes. She asked me where on earth I had been for the last hour, and told me they'd assumed that I had been doing a round on my own, until I buzzed for aid from a member of staff. It was then that I looked down at my fob watch; and was shocked to see that it was almost 2 a.m.! The strange thing was that to me, I had just arrived up there, and had just run away from those two strange beings at the end of the corridor to hide in the bathroom.

They were definitely not human, having large pointed ears, large noses, no hair that I could see, and a leathery-looking skin, which appeared to be a dull brown colour. The male's eyes were red, and I found him very frightening.

May said that I looked very pale and asked what had happened. I told her what I had seen, but I think she thought I was hallucinating or something, because she went to have a look down the corridor and couldn't find a sign of anyone! She then insisted on making me a cup of sweet tea, the English answer to shock; and obviously, this strange occurrence was shared with the other staff, including the nursing assistants, who proceeded to tease me to death about it. They all, bizarrely, put it down to my seeing more ghosts, and failed to hear or comprehend me when I described the pair's strange appearance.

This incident, and the fact that it actually happened whilst I was at work, scared me a lot, because 'they' had never 'taken' me before in that way, up until that point, or at least not that I could recall—apart from the possible exception of the strange interview in the city office.

Frighteningly, it came home to me then that I could be taken from anywhere and at any time! What I really wanted to know though was, *why me*, and why at that time? I had no answer.

Chapter 7

I meet my second husband, get engaged, move house and undergo some more strange experiences

Shortly after this incident, I met my second husband.

During 1994, nothing more happened, and I was left alone to get on with my life. By this time, I had found a room in a shared house, and made a good friend, who I frequently went out with — I met my second husband whilst I was out with her.

1995

In 1995, I got engaged, and I moved in with my fiancé. We bought a nice semi-detached house (duplex) together, at the end of a cul-de-sac — it had a large lounge and a through dining room which led off to the kitchen. There were French windows leading off the dining room, and we worked hard to get the overgrown garden back into something resembling order. We built a small wall at the end of the back garden and planted flower seeds along it, which eventually bloomed. We tidied up the side garden too, and laid some new lawn which grew quickly. I also reclaimed a number of rose bushes that had gone to seed, trimming them in the hope that they would recover and flower, and to my surprise, they did!

A total power outage occurs: Summer 1995

While my fiancé was away on a shift one night, during the summer of 1995, there was a total power outage during the night, and I was very scared, because I could hear voices coming from the garden, but I just froze with fear in my bed.

Then I heard a voice in my head, in the form of what I can only describe as a telepathic request. A voice literally entered my head, asking me to go down to the garden. These are the words I heard: *"Come to the back garden, come now!"*

Sadly, I did not then have the courage to move, and I just tried to ignore this voice, but then I heard—what by now—I recognized as the pre-abduction noise of buzzing, and my body became paralyzed from top to toe, and I felt a strong vibration passing through me, then seemed to black out, and I did not come to again until morning.

Relieved that it was light, I got out of bed and visited the bathroom. It was still early, around 6 a.m., so I went back to bed, and I had a very vivid dream of the night before.

I dreamt that I got out of bed in the nightdress I was wearing in reality: a white cotton one, and I went to the top of the stairs to find a man waiting at the bottom of the stairs for me. He was very tall, at least 7 feet plus, and was dressed in what looked like a dark navy-blue diving suit, tight-fitting from top to toe. His mouth and nose were covered with a mask, but I could see his eyes, which were very striking, being deep blue and wraparound, larger than ours, sloe-shaped, with larger pupils, more like a cat's eyes than a human's and slanting upwards. (See my drawing below.)

He beckoned to me to come down the stairs towards him, and I went down, seemingly without fear, and I remember that his large eyes looked friendly, as if trying to reassure me that he meant me no harm. Then I woke up, and this dream struck me as singularly odd, because, of course, it reminded me of what had happened with regard to the voices in my head.

For the next few nights following this dream, I started to have vivid flashbacks, like stills from a film, of witnessing my dining-room ceiling, just at the bottom of the stairs, open up to reveal a row of what looked like four Tic-Tac-shaped shiny black craft, standing on a very shiny black flooring against the backdrop of an equally plain, highly polished, very shiny black wall.

I also recalled being escorted down a corridor where guards saluted me and someone who was with me. I couldn't see this individual, but I knew I was being escorted. These guards seemed to be saluting whoever was with me by pressing the flat of their right hands to their shoulder as we went past. Their uniforms were tight-fitting and also navy blue. I can only remember the top part of them; they looked like tight-fitting diver's suits with tight turtleneck collars that I think were black, and there was an insignia on them on the left breast, but I can't recall what it looked like. There were no females present that I can recall. These men had uniform features, high cheekbones, dark hair, and olive skin, and reminded me, with their features, of people that come from the Maori tribe of New Zealand, though with larger sloe-shaped eyes.

The alien visitor that I saw at the bottom of my stairs.

I also remember seeing what I can only describe as the Celtic cross and the fleur-de-lis symbol carved into the corridor walls. I remember being very struck by these, as I am particularly interested in Celtic culture, being of Celtic origin myself, my father being from Scotland and a red-haired, blue-eyed Scot!

I tried to tell my husband about all this, but he couldn't, or wouldn't, understand, and put it down to my having a vivid imagination, just as my mum had done years before. So I was left to cope with these traumatic events alone.

Moreover, on subsequent nights following this incident, although I did not have flashbacks, I did, I believe, continue to get taken, as the paralysis episodes continued. When this happened, I would scream in my head to my sleeping inert partner for help, but there would be no response, and then it would suddenly be early morning and light within seconds!

This made me feel quite upset at times, and I became suicidal and was put on antidepressants for some time.

In addition to this, there was a strange incident with the little boy next door, whose backyard was adjacent to our garden at that time. He said to my partner (who incidentally put it down to pranking) that I was seeing another man while he was away on night shifts; and that he had seen this man climbing in through the back spare-room window! To this day, I have no idea what this kid was talking about! Could he have seen something that he shouldn't have seen in connection with these mysterious visitors?

A suspect and dark stranger

Also, about a week after the events related above, I was visited by an ordinary but good-looking guy with a dark tanned complexion and dark-brown hair; he looked perfectly normal, but his energy felt 'off' to me, as if he was hiding something.

This man knocked on my door, just as I was about to go shopping. He then asked me a very strange question pertaining to my father's surname. Following this event, I had to ask myself how a complete stranger would know about, or manage to make a reference to, my maiden name.

The question was: "Are you connected to the McAdam family?"

At the time, this did not occur to me as anything out of the ordinary, but when I look back on it, it seems very suspicious indeed. Also, he let me see him get into a long black sports car that looked brand new. I regret that I did not think to get the number plate, or note the type of car, other than that it was some kind of sports car.

All of these incidents coming together in a short time, in the summer of 1995, from June through to September of that year, left me feeling very puzzled and confused and also scared and depressed.

Some facts about my Scottish surname:

- My family coat of arms has the fleur-de-lis in it.
- We originate from Celtic/Norman French ancestors.
- We are from the Lowlands around Dumfries and Galloway.
- We are a branch of Clan Gregor and the De Gordons.
- We also have connections to Ireland.

Could any of this be relevant to my ET experiences? I have no idea!

Chapter 8

1997–2007: Visited during pregnancy, difficult births, two sons, and a suspect encounter in Tenerife

Nothing more out of the ordinary happened after that, until I became pregnant with my first child, a boy.

While I was carrying him, 'they' seemed to take me several times over the course of my pregnancy. The baby was never harmed, as far as I know, but the paralysis and buzzing sensations and the sense of knowing I was being taken started again, and I lived in fear for my unborn child.

I have one vivid memory of seeing them on one occasion; this one looked like one of the typical 'Grays' as depicted on the cover of Whitley Strieber's *Communion*. I was having an afternoon nap during my second trimester, and I woke to find him standing over me with an iron-shaped object in his hand. I was also paralyzed, and I swore at him in my head, telling him to go—and not in a polite way! Of course, I blacked out, and it was late afternoon when I came to.

My pregnancy was a difficult one, and my son went two weeks over term. In the end, I could not deliver him by the natural means and I underwent an emergency caesarean section. Following this, I became very ill with an infection and was unable to breastfeed, which led to me getting severe postnatal depression. It took me at least two months to recover from giving birth, but once I did, I started to enjoy being a new mum.

Strangely, as soon as the baby was born, the paralysis and buzzing episodes abated, and it seemed that I was left alone again.

Later on, at the age of just six, my son got a diagnosis of

Asperger's syndrome and was also thought to be highly intelligent. He was classed as a gifted child at school, and his IQ was off the scale.

He hated being parted from me, and it wrenched at my heart leaving him every day at primary school. However, as he got older, this got less severe, and he learned to cope without me.

Today, he is very antisocial, due to the Asperger's, but very loving nonetheless with family and close friends. He is 24 now and works as a computer engineer, which suits his disposition. He has the mind of a professor, and has gained a first-class degree and a distinction at Master's level in his subject area.

While my husband and I were undoubtedly clever people, and I realize that intelligence can be passed on, I have to wonder about my first son being so extremely clever. He has never needed to study and has breezed through all his exams with no particular effort on his part, and we have been surprised that he has done as well as he has. Intelligence is not an effort for him; it is his gift. I have to wonder if 'they' had something to do with this.

Significantly, he has never reported any encounters or what he thought of as abduction experiences. I say this because I have shared at length my own experiences with him, and although he is mystified by them, he does believe me. He does not profess to have had any experiences of abduction.

After he was born, nothing more happened for a while, and we moved house, close to Scotland due to my husband relocating for his job. Then, for four years we lived on a new housing estate in a small village.

Nothing more happened in the two years between 1998 and 2000, except that I got pregnant with my second child, another son, in late 2000.

As with my first son, the frightening experiences of what I now believe was abduction started up again. I can vividly remember being taken in my middle trimester, when I actually came to, in the early morning, in my kitchen, and I noted it had just turned 4 a.m. when I looked at the kitchen clock—I wondered if I had merely sleepwalked on that occasion.

But the following night I had a very vivid dream, or recall of this event, and I dreamt that someone had asked me down to the kitchen. I couldn't see them, but they had gently taken hold of me from behind, and I felt I was about to be examined or checked up on. This frightened me, considering what I had gone through before, during my first pregnancy.

I gave birth to my second son via elective caesarean section, and this time I recovered more quickly. Once again, I suffered with postnatal depression and was treated for this.

The strange experiences that had occurred during my pregnancy stopped as well, and I breathed a sigh of relief about that.

Once my scars had healed, I took up learning to drive, as it was very difficult to lug around a large toddler (my first son), a pram, and a newborn baby. I was desperate to pass my driving test.

We only had one car at that point, so I was obliged to use the bus if I wanted to go into the nearby town. I only did this if a friend came with me, or when my mum came to stay, as it was so difficult without being able to drive.

When my second son was six months old, I passed my driving test, and my husband bought me a little old banger, a Fiat, which I loved because of the newfound independence that it gave me.

2001

In 2001, we moved house again to a larger house with more rooms. This house needed a lot of alterations as it was old and neglected. However, we both had sufficient imagination to see how it could look, and we got it at a bargain price.

Moving from a new house to this old one was depressing for me, but we soon set to, decorating it, and we also put in a new bathroom at the front.

Meanwhile, my first son was enrolled in the local village school, and started school, while my younger son stayed at home with me.

We had three lovely garden spaces at this house, and during the summer I would let my younger son, who walked at quite a late age, move about on his bottom in the walled-off side garden. He loved to play with his toys on the lawn in the sunshine, and I would watch him and wait until school pickup time. Then I would place him in his little pushchair and we would go and pick up my eldest from school.

I am relieved to report that, for some time, I was left alone to live my ordinary mundane life, which was largely looking after my two sons, doing the housework, shopping, and picking the children up from nursery and school.

The youngest eventually started school too, and I made the most of the free time by joining an art group (all the drawings in this book are mine), as I have always had a talent for drawing and painting, and I did manage to sell some of my work via this local group.

Later—July 2007: Tenerife

We decided to have two weeks away, as my husband and I were both feeling worn out with work and housework, and felt we deserved a well-earned break. So, we arranged a holiday to Tenerife.

Nothing untoward happened during the holiday, except that the boys were constantly bickering with each other. I suppose this is how most siblings are, though, and in spite of this, we managed to have a nice holiday.

During the holiday, my husband took the children out for days without me, and I really appreciated this, as it gave me a break from them; I would sit on a sun lounger, reading a book and enjoying the peace. It was only at the end of this trip that I was to meet a somewhat 'suspect' stranger.

The boys were quite young at the time and had been constantly fighting and getting on my nerves. Consequently, on the day of departure, I developed a very bad migraine and was sick on the coach going to the airport.

My husband visited the chemist and bought me some medication over the counter that cured the migraine within minutes, although it did leave me feeling very dopey.

He then left me and took the boys to buy them a toy each, which was always a tradition of ours on holidays. Meanwhile, I sat in the seating area close to the airport shops and waited for them.

Suddenly, a white-haired man, who looked about 60 in age, sat next to me, and immediately I felt that his energy was that of a wise old elder, while also feeling that he was somehow not of this world. Well, this man proceeded to get my attention by staring intently at me, and I couldn't help saying "Hello" out of embarrassment.

Suddenly, he started giving me advice about, of all things, my youngest son! The strange thing was, I never stopped to ask myself how on earth he could possibly know me at all, or know enough about my family, to be in a position to offer advice to me. The advice was specifically about the youngest, and it was the sort of thing that a grandfather might say about an unruly grandson.

He said, and I quote: "You need to stop letting him be the big boss, or you will regret it. I see you had a migraine with them playing you up on the coach—no wonder."

I also thought nothing of arguing the point with him. "He is not the big boss!" I replied indignantly.

"Yes he is, and you are letting him be the boss. You should chastise him more!"

At this point, he got up and walked off, and I can honestly say that as soon as he departed, the absurdity of the situation suddenly did strike me; it was very odd indeed.

When my husband returned with the boys, clutching toy airplanes, I immediately told him about this encounter, but he just dismissed it as some nosey old person poking their nose in where it clearly wasn't wanted, and dismissed the high strangeness of it.

But I have never forgotten this encounter, and frankly, it has haunted me for years. There are so many questions that it brings up:

- Who was this man?
- Why did he have a distinctly foreign accent which sounded Germanic in tone?
- Why did he care enough about me to comment on my youngest son's behavior?
- How did he know that I had just recovered from a migraine?
- Why did his energy feel strange?

Why did I also observe the following things about his appearance?

- He had very large, watery blue eyes.
- He had very pale, almost white skin, in a place were everyone was tanned from the sun.
- He had very pale white hair.

Now, you could suggest that he might have been on the airport departure coach, but there were very few people on there, and all of them would have been British guests, because the coach was specifically for those catching the UK flight. However, he had a Germanic accent.

Moreover, before I got ill on the coach, I had carefully looked around me, as I am by nature a people watcher and always observant of others around me; there was definitely no one who had looked like this man on the coach!

Chapter 9

2008, July–August: More UFO sightings, an invitation to "Come and meet us," and missing time at the cinema

Events in early July 2008: a strange dream

During this month, I had a strange dream, and this dream was very vivid.

I dreamt that a small Tic-Tac-shaped, cream-colored craft, about the size of an average car, had landed in my front garden. In my dream, I got out of bed, opened my front door, and went across the garden to meet a handsome blond-haired man, who looked no older than 28 at most — again thinking of the 'Nordic' aliens here. He had climbed out through a door on the side of this craft and was waiting there to greet me. After this I woke up, but unusually I have never forgotten this dream, for reasons I will go on to outline.

Two days later, I was driving back from the library with my husband, as we often took the children to pick books in order to encourage them to read — when to the right of our car, in the lower field down the road from our house, my husband pointed at some strange crop formations that had appeared there. We stopped the car on my request and got out to examine these formations, and they were in the shape of a capital H and the swastika.

My husband, who is normally very cynical and very scientific, went into the field to take a closer look, and he had to conclude that the markings could have only come from something landing there, as there were no footprints, except his own on the wet grass.

Moreover, when we climbed out of this field, we noticed that a Land Rover with blacked-out windows was waiting nearby, and it felt very much as if the driver was waiting for us to go, which we did. We did not have any cameras or phones capable of taking photos with us at that time, so no, we did not take photos.

When we arrived at our home, an amazing thing happened: there was also a black Land Rover parked on our drive, and being annoyed by someone's cheekiness, we both looked to see who was driving it, or at least I did, since my husband was concentrating on his driving.

The strange thing was that the driver of this vehicle looked just like the man I had greeted in my dream a few days earlier, being blond, handsome, and frankly, Nordic-looking. He had a woman with him, also blond with long hair, who was very pretty and also looked Nordic in appearance. When they noticed us, they looked surprised, and quickly got out of our drive and drove off. I felt very stunned by this, but I did not share with my husband about the dream I had experienced, because I really don't think he would have believed me about the man in the vehicle looking identical to the one in my dream.

Oh the irony!

During July of this same year, my family and I went on a trip to the cinema in order to watch the film *The X-Files: I Want to Believe*. Anyone who has read up to here will have no need to ask why I was very eager to watch this particular film, especially if they have also seen the series.

When the *X-Files* series came out during the 1990s, the contents really resonated with me, and I could also empathize with its central character, Fox Mulder, whose abduction experiences and search for the truth closely mirrored some of my own real-life experiences.

While I realize that this series was fictional, its writer, Chris Carter, has stated the following with reference to his series:

The plot of "The X-Files" was built on a conspiracy theory: The government is lying to you about the existence of U.F.O.s and extraterrestrials. Do I believe the government lies to us? Absolutely. I'm a child of Watergate.[3]

In addition, he had this to say on the subject of abduction, as reported by Professor John E. Mack during his extensive research into this area of the ET phenomenon. When the writer observed for himself an abductee under hypnosis, interacting with the professor, he made the following observation:

In 1996 I was invited to the clinic of the Harvard psychiatrist John Mack to witness the regression hypnosis of a self-professed alien abductee. I first met Dr. Mack, who studied and ultimately believed in alien abduction, when he came to Fox Studios to discuss his work. I had used a Roper survey he was involved in (a poll of 6000 Americans on their belief in the existence of extraterrestrials) to sell "The X-Files" as a TV show in 1992, and later read his book, "Abduction." So I knew something about what I was going to see. I went in doubtful, unprepared for the drama of a woman sitting next to me in tears and in terror over the encounter with aliens that she described, on a beach in Mexico. The experience turned out to be powerful and not a little unsettling.[4]

I have reported this here in order to show that, although *The X-Files* was indeed fictional, the series' creator had arguably based some of its contents on what he had observed of Professor John E. Mack's work with this abductee, and he was obviously greatly moved by what he had observed of this particular person. Therefore, it is not unreasonable to argue that the series would no doubt resonate with abductees around the world—in essence with those whose experiences have been similar to the ones I relate in this book.

It was ironic, therefore, that I should go missing, at least from the perspective of my family, for approximately 30 minutes following our watching of the film based on this series. This event took place around the ladies' bathroom at the cinema; this was the Vue Cinema in a minor city in Cumbria, UK—a perfectly ordinary cinema with several screens and seating areas.

Following the film, I excused myself from my family group and went into the ladies' toilets. The only strange thing that I can recall was that on entering the toilets, there was nobody present but me, and this was very unusual, since it has never happened before. In fact, in my past experience, there had always been a queue for the toilets following a film. Not so on this occasion! In addition to this, on entering the toilets, the lights above me suddenly flickered on and off, and they did this a number of times, as from my perspective I immediately chose a cubicle and made myself comfortable in there.

Then, following what to me was a brief five-minute visit, I emerged from there to find my husband and boys waving at me in an angry fashion. Wondering what on earth could be wrong, I went over to them. On reaching them, my husband pointed to his watch and angrily asked me what on earth I had been doing for the past half an hour. To say that I was shocked by this question is something of an understatement, and I immediately looked at my own watch in order to refute this. However, on looking at my watch, I discovered that it had mysteriously stopped at the wrong time, and that my husband's watch did indeed show that at least half an hour had passed. I was so baffled, at the time, that I failed to take in the seriousness of this event, or what it implied, especially given my history in this area.

I wish I had taken note of the date and time of this event, but retrospect is a great thing, and it is only due to my husband reminding me about this strange incident years later, while I was writing this book, that I have remembered it at all. However, my two boys and my husband witnessed this and got very annoyed at the time, saying that from their perspective I had taken half an hour at least; while from my own, I had only taken five minutes. As the Americans say: Go figure!

August 2008: Strange lights over the fields

It was now the middle of August 2008, and I was feeling very hot. We had experienced an unusually hot summer, with the temperatures, at times, mirroring those of Spain. I had opened my bedroom windows and left the curtains open to try and get some fresh air in, but it was too hot and I could not sleep, so I got out of bed with the intention of making myself a cup of tea, when my eyes caught sight of some lights over the field in front of our house.

As I looked at the far field, behind the bushes in the distance, a number of strange lights, bright white in colour, quickly came apart, then came back together again. Fascinated, I watched these for some time, until they suddenly went out; then I decided it was probably some kids playing jokes with flashlights and went back to bed with a glass of water.

About an hour later, I was woken up by a loud humming noise, which sounded like there was a helicopter or something huge over the house. I ran to the window to see what was overhead and was amazed to see a round object in the same field! It was cylindrical in shape (see drawing included in this chapter) and looked as big as two buses in my estimation, and moreover, as I watched, it rolled on its side like a wheel. It looked enormous, and there were orange and green lights intermittently flashing along the sides of this thing. So, I watched it for a few minutes, until the lights suddenly went out and it just seemed to disappear! You may assume that I would have run to wake the boys, or my husband, but being very tired indeed by now, I just went back to bed and went back to sleep, even though I was feeling somewhat shocked by all of this. Why on earth, having seen this huge craft, was I so calm?

I did tell my husband the next day, vowing and also warning him that, if these lights appeared again over that field, I would drive nearer to get a closer look. He laughed and said that if he heard me drive off in the middle of the night, he would not get too worried, unless I failed to return. He then started to take 'the mickey' somewhat and commenced humming the tune to *The Twilight Zone*, which earned him a withering look from me!

Two days later: August 2008

Two days later, I was obliged to carry out my threat, as the lights did return. This time it was the zigzagging white lights, and I immediately got changed and went to get in my car. Looking at the car's clock, I saw that it was 3:15 a.m. Feeling very scared, and somewhat foolish, I made my way towards the M6 junction of the motorway, taking the road out of the village towards the roundabout.

I had got halfway down this road, when to my right, at the bottom of the long drive that leads down from the field where I had witnessed the lights previously, I saw that there was now a stationary pearl-colored, egg-shaped craft (see drawing included in this chapter) parked there off the B6263 (a minor road). I assumed it was some sort of craft anyway—I have never seen anything like this before or since! I estimate that it was about the size of two large cars on top of each other, it was cream in color, and looked pearly in the night light, as if it was lit up from inside. I don't remember seeing windows, but there was a door in the middle of it, and in front of this open door, or gap, stood two figures in silhouette. I could not for some reason make out their features, but they were both very tall, thin, and proud-looking in their bearing. I also felt that they were male, and that they were waiting for me.

By this time, I had pulled to the side of the road, but fear prevented me from getting out of the car to take a closer look. At the time, all sorts of things went through my head such as: *Are they going to abduct me if I get out of my car?* Also: *Is my car going to start again?* In the event, I got the engine started, and I drove off towards the M6 South exit in a real panic! To this day, I don't know why I took the motorway exit. I was by now, though, in great shock and definitely not thinking straight!

Significantly, as I entered the motorway feeder road, a tall blond man tried to wave me down. He was to my right on the edge of the road, and he wore ordinary clothes, pale chinos, a light summer jacket and a shirt, and he was waiting on the grass verge that bordered the feeder road, but I did not stop. I was too scared, and I now found myself on the M6 and had no option but to head for the nearby service station, where I thought I could pull in and calm down a bit.

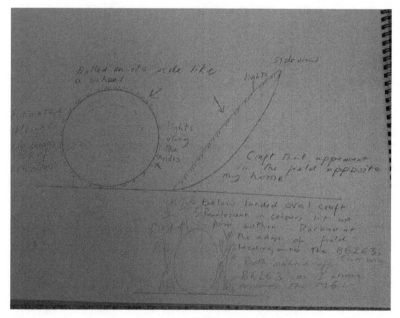

I was so confused and scared by then that my hands were shaking, so I pulled into a layby close to the service station, only to notice what appeared to be a white lorry (truck) parked about 50 yards to my left. Thinking that the driver might know of a turn off that led back onto the M6 North, and still feeling panicky, I got out of my car and went towards this plain white lorry, which strangely had no logos or number plates that I can recall.

A tall man emerged from the cabin and stepped down onto the tarmac. He had wavy short strawberry-blond hair, and was quite handsome in appearance. Strangely, it was as if he was waiting for me! I ran up to him and asked him how you turn around for the northern M6 motorway, since I was on the south side, and he didn't speak at all, but just gestured to me to follow him in his lorry. So, instinctively trusting him, I got back in my car, and followed what appeared to be the back end of this white lorry, but there was no rumbling truck-engine sound as he set off, and I found this strange in retrospect. I followed him for at least ten minutes and I felt as if we crossed over a bridge. He then sped up and left me to it, or so it seemed from my perspective.

When I got back home at 5 a.m. — and this in itself was unusual as this journey usually takes 20 minutes at most — my husband asked me where I had been. I told him what had happened, but I don't think he believed me; he made out that I had been following Chinese lanterns. This was definitely not the case!

Thinking about this 'lorry' afterwards — although I have never been hypnotically regressed back to that night — I now suspect that it was not a lorry at all, but some kind of craft that I was made to think was a lorry, because when I drove back to that same service station, there was definitely no way to turn around and head back north at all! To head back north you have to drive further south to the next M6 junction! This is definitely the case.

So what happened to me that night? This is what I think really happened: I believe I was rescued by the same people who had earlier attempted to get me to approach their visible craft (see above). For some reason, they cared enough to come and rescue me off the M6, knowing that I was in a bad state! Why do I now think this? Because there is just no other explanation, that's why. There is no turning road at the service station I pulled into that would get me back going north. I have since checked it is blocked, and even if you got around the block, there is no road bridge!

The lorry was plain white with no visible logos. I have never seen a lorry with no logos, have you? Additionally, I have since recalled some of the event back, and remember seeing a white wall in front of my car, so close that there is no way that my car was following that lorry, or it would have collided with it! I believe that what I have recalled was my temporarily being taken up into some kind of white-walled holding bay, until it was safe to put me back down onto the motorway. Also, the man did not say anything to me; he merely gestured at me. Have you ever met a silent lorry driver?

The events of that night continue to haunt me, and more was to follow, as you will see.

"Come and meet us!"

A few weeks later, I was telepathically contacted by a male voice in my head, and asked to go to a meeting. I was given the time of 1 p.m., and told that I would be met at Waterstones booksellers in my local town, in the coffee shop, and that they would approach me. This happened in the now late August of that year, 2008. I did not note the exact date and deeply regret that I didn't now.

Intrigued, and feeling a little stupid—wondering in fact if I was going mad—I obeyed these instructions to the letter, and promptly sat down in the Waterstones café at 1 p.m. with a latte.

To my utter astonishment, two young people approached my table and sat down adjacent to me. They both wore identical navy-blue overalls like those that mechanics wear, with no visible logos or badges, and what looked like tight-fitting black boots with no laces; these were also identical. One was a woman, and I estimate that they were both no more than 20 years old. The young woman was very pale skinned and had large pale-blue eyes, with blond, slightly wavy mid-length hair. The young man, in contrast, was Asiatic-looking, had dark brown skin, and very large brown eyes, unusually large, a thing that struck me at the time. I attempted to telepathically contact them by saying a greeting in my head, and the woman nodded at me, letting me know, I believe, that she had heard me. They did not order coffee, and specifically asked for orange juice too—I wonder if they consider coffee bad for them? They didn't say anything to me out loud at all during this brief exchange. Strangely, after I had greeted them, they both got up, abandoned their orange drinks, and made for the shop exit. I followed them, but when I emerged from the shop just seconds after them, they had disappeared completely, which struck me as odd, since there is no way they could have got away from there and out of sight so fast!

So here was another mystery for me. I still remember this pair, years later, and can't think for the life of me why they initiated this meeting, unless it really was only to say: *"Here we are! You were not imagining things after all, nor are you going mad, and we can contact you telepathically at any time!"*

Following this memorable year, I was left alone for a long time, eight years in fact, when nothing out of the ordinary happened to me at all, and I honestly didn't mind, as I never wanted or looked for this to happen to me.

Chapter 10

July 28, 2016: High strangeness in Tenerife during our summer holiday

In the summer of 2016 we went on holiday to Los Christianos, Tenerife, and on the second day of the holiday we went to Los Christianos beach. My husband went off for a walk with the boys and left me to sunbathe on this busy beach.

Now, I have Spanish ancestry on my matriarchal side, and although I have my father's fairer complexion (Dad is Celtic), my skin also has olive overtones from my mum; so, normally, I don't burn easily at all, even without using sunscreen.

For example, in 1976, during the searing heatwave that swept across the UK, I went about all day in my swimsuit and shorts without sunscreen, and my skin did not burn—I just gradually became brown.

In 1978, when I was just 14, I twice went on holiday to destinations where it was very hot and sunny. I visited a friend in southern France and merely turned brown, with no sunscreen!

I also spent two weeks in Cornwall, camping in another heatwave, without sunscreen, and my father, who did burn, and proceeded to become sore and red, necessitating the use of aftersun cream, remarked how annoying it was that I proceeded always to merely turn brown, gradually turning a lovely dark color in any type of sun!

My brother, who has Dad's sensitive Celtic skin, also burned red in the sun, and when he comes on holidays with us now, he still uses liberal amounts of sunscreen.

Moreover, I had applied sunscreen that day—as there is more awareness of the need to protect your skin in these more recent times than there was during the 1970s; and knowing how hot it was at the beach, this was only sensible.

However, when my husband returned to pick me up, I was surprised when he informed me that it was close to lunchtime already, since when I arrived, it had only just turned 9:30 a.m.— because I did check my watch to see how long I had before he promised to return at 12ish.

When I stood up to get my beach trousers on, my husband gave me a shocked look and asked me pointedly why I had not used sunscreen, because I was now badly burned on my neck, and strangely, I had massive hand-shaped burns to my inner thighs, which had not even been in the sun, being under a parasol, and also I had liberally applied sunscreen to them, as I pointed out.

Moreover, I could not now account for how quickly the time had passed, which left me feeling very confused, and I pointed out to my husband how surprised I was that it was lunchtime already; but he just said that I must have fallen asleep! However, from my point of view, I will swear that I did not fall asleep, and that I had only been there for half an hour!

Well, as the day went on, these burns just got worse and worse, and I ended up calling the doctor out, who gave me some cream for them, and this helped, but the burns and scarring to my legs would take weeks to go! Moreover, I felt nauseated and generally off for months afterwards.

There were also large red handprints across both of my thighs, and these grew very sore over the following days and started to peel and discharge pus! The hands looked like a human-shaped hand, but the fingers were very thin and long. I regret that I did not photograph my thighs; I can only put this omission down to the fact that I was feeling so ill!

I only have a photo of my upper burns due to my husband taking a family photo of me on an excursion we went on a few days later, after I had been given painkillers and burn-numbing cream from the doctor that came out to see me.

I really feel as if something significant must have happened to me on the beach that day, as nothing like that has happened either before or since, because as I say: *I do not sunburn easily!* As a general rule of thumb! Moreover, since this event, I have walked about all day in strong hot Florida sunshine, having my sunscreen fail, due to sweating issues, and I have still not burned.

So what happened? I have come to the conclusion that I was abducted that day, somehow in broad daylight, from a busy beach without anyone noticing! This is not impossible for 'them.' Go and google "People abducted by ETs from busy places."

Yes, my supposition sounds incredible, even to me! Also, I am going to surmise that, somehow, they made a mistake and forgot to turn something off or on, and that my severe sunburn and subsequent illness was the result. I have no other explanation at all for this event.

In addition to the burns, when I eventually got to sleep that night, I had an extremely vivid and suspect dream, and this is what I dreamt.

I suddenly found myself inside some kind of craft. I was strapped into a seat and unable to move, while everything around me was white. I remember looking over to my right and seeing a dark-haired woman with short hair, who looked very much like us, with one exception: she had extremely large dark-brown eyes and stared back at me, her eyes conveying fear and confusion all at the same time.

Then the scene switched, and I found myself in a field and someone was chasing me, and when I looked behind me, it was this same very tall, dark-haired young woman, who eventually caught up to me and attempted to give me a hug, but why? Meanwhile, I was able to study this landscape, and it was very much like Earth, except for one crucial difference: the sun there was not as strong. Simply put, even though I felt it was afternoon, the light there was akin to our twilight or early sunset.

Then suddenly the scene switched again, and I was talking

with a pale-skinned, blond-haired man who took me inside some kind of vehicle that flew up, and suddenly we were over huge ice fields, with an ice wall to one side of me.

After this, I woke up. I found this dream very disturbing, and I have remembered it in detail ever since. I have often wondered if I was seeing myself in a future or a past life on another world, similar to Earth, but with a weaker sun. I can still remember the flat landscape that stretched for miles and the pale-blue sky lit up by this weak sun, and I had to wonder if my earlier traumatic experiences of the day were in fact linked with this very vivid dream, or a possible recall of something important to me or my identity.

Thankfully, the rest of 2016 went off without any more suspicious happenings, and I believe that I was left alone until the momentous year that was going to be 2020, the year of Covid-19 and lockdowns.

I have since conducted research on burns and sunburns associated with UFOs and abductions, and I have found documented evidence that people all over the planet have received third-degree burns and worse from close contacts with UFOs, either through getting too near them, or during remembered abductions. Just put the words "Burned by UFO" into any good search engine, and you will see this for yourself.

Of course, I could be entirely wrong, but if I take all of the circumstantial evidence into consideration, I have to wonder if I was abducted that day, because as God is my witness, I have never burned that badly in the sun either before or since this incident!

Whether people believe me of course is for them to decide. That is their privilege, and frankly, I don't really care one way or the other, as the purpose of this book is to tell the truth as it happened to me, in the most honest way that I am able to recall events. You may want to argue that I merely fell asleep, but consider this: I believe I would remember that. That leaves a considerable amount of missing time to account for—more than two hours!

Also, I have to stress again that due to my mother's fortunate genes, *I do not burn easily in the sun.* This was the first and only time in my life when I have been burned so badly that I blistered, and those blisters oozed for days afterwards!

In addition, I felt very ill and 'off' for weeks following this, with nausea, extreme tiredness, a constant thirst, and an upset stomach. This is not normal in the case of ordinary sunburns.

Chapter 11

2020: Three strange spots appear on my arm and an interloper appears in my bedroom

In the January of a newly dawned 2020, my husband and I were able to go on holiday as a couple for the first time in years, as both our sons were away at university and sharing a house together. The youngest was a first-year undergraduate, and the eldest was completing a Master's degree.

The Covid-19 virus hit the nearby island of Lanzarote as we holidayed in Tenerife, and neither of us considered then the monumental impact that this awful 'virus' was about to have.

By February of that year, we began to watch the news with fear as we saw how bad the situation had become in Italy, with the virus infecting a large proportion of the population, putting considerable pressure on the Italian health services.

I watched this with trepidation, surmising that it would only be a matter of time before the 'virus' hit the UK. Sure enough, it soon did, and before we knew it the first lockdown had begun in the March of that year.

The only silver lining during this lockdown was the hot sunny weather, and my family and I went on lots of local walks in the nearby fields.

I struggled to cope with visits to the supermarket, where at first it was hard to get hold of simple household items like toilet rolls. In fact, I can even remember feeling lucky to find packets of these at Bargain Booze!

However, once people stopped panic buying, I soon grew used to disinfecting my hands at the front of shops and wearing a mask, although I have to say that due to my having asthma, I never really felt comfortable wearing masks, and would often have an asthma attack on removing them.

I believe that ET contact and some form of abduction started happening again during this year, and I believe it began in the form of a voice that I heard in my head warning me what was about to happen: *"You are going to go through a very difficult time, but we are going to protect you."*

This happened during the night, in fact, on the first of April. I couldn't get to sleep and kept tossing and turning in bed. Suddenly, I was paralyzed again, but there was no accompanying buzzing sound this time, just the paralysis, and then I heard this voice coming from behind me telling me this.

I somehow managed to break free from the paralysis— maybe they hadn't got a good enough fix on my determined personage that night—so I was able to turn around in bed, and to my immediate right I could just make out the shape of a tall figure in the dark who was standing with their left side facing me. I felt this person was male, and I saw that he had shoulder-length hair, but I couldn't see what color it was. He was also very tall, at least 6 feet—as my eldest son, who is this tall, has also stood on that side of the bed, so I could estimate the person's height from this. Also, he wore some kind of dark overall which was long, like the kurta commonly worn by men of Indian ethnicity. I could not see his lower garments, but obviously the bed was in the way of my seeing either trousers or footwear. I'm not sure whether he allowed me to see him or whether it was an accident; but when I gasped with fear, as I took all this in within a few seconds, he quickly just faded out or disappeared.

Later, still sensing a presence in my room, I just pointed my camera into the darkness and took a photo (photos available on request from the author: See author's email on back page). If you look at it, you can clearly see that there is a tall figure (I suspect the same male) standing on the left of the photo, and he is very tall, since my dressing-table mirror is to one side of him, and his height is well above it.

I quickly reached for my bedside lamp switch following this, and of course when the light came on there was nothing to see out of the ordinary. This left me wondering if I had just dreamt the whole thing. However, taken together with the voice, and the words that I had heard coming from outside me, or so it felt, I have to wonder about this.

Shortly after this, again feeling that there was a presence in my bedroom, I decided that I would try an experiment with my phone recorder and craftily switched it on. To my surprise, on playing it back, I had caught someone saying "No!" in an angry tone; the voice was definitely male. I still have this recording on my phone.

For the rest of April, nothing at all happened out of the ordinary, until one night at the beginning of May. I went to bed as usual, and it seemed that no sooner had I shut my eyes than I was waking up to daylight, and it was exactly 7 a.m. when I checked the time with my mobile phone.

Moreover, my lower left arm felt sore at the bottom, and when I examined it, I found three tiny red puncture marks that, if joined, would form a triangle shape. These marks had not been there before. They have since faded. (See photo below.)

I didn't think anything of these marks when I first saw them. Because they were itchy and sore, I just put it down to having been bitten by some kind of insect, as I often sit in the garden reading or listening to music. Thinking this was nothing out of the ordinary, I did not take a photo of them at the time when they were red and sore.

However, towards the end of June, I woke up to another voice. This time, it seemed to come from inside my head, although it's very hard to describe this phenomenon. I clearly heard a male voice say that the marks I had found were due to *"a necessary medical procedure."* There was no further explanation forthcoming as to what, or why, this procedure had been carried out, and I actually found myself wondering once again if I was in fact going mad, or hallucinating, or if I'd dreamt it. But those marks were clearly there; that could not be denied! How they got there is open to question, and I do realize that a lot of people will dismiss them out of hand as insect bites, but what insects bite to form a perfect triangle? I have to say that, in all honesty, I wish I could believe that they were just bites, as the other possibility is frankly quite unnerving to say the least!

In addition, I am by no means alone in coming away from

These marks appeared on my skin due to "a necessary medical procedure." They seem to form a triangle shape. They have since faded out.

these strange experiences with unexplained scars or marks on me. When I conducted research following this incident, I quickly realized that the appearance of sites of injury, or scar tissue, caused by possible medical procedures is a well-documented area in the abductee body of evidence.

(For more about this, I would recommend reading *Casebook: Alien Implants* by Roger Leir.)

Chapter 12

More high strangeness in July on holiday in Kent (2020) and Skegness (2021)

At the beginning of July 2020, due to a relaxation of England's lockdown rules, we decided to have a short holiday in Kent. We set off, and everything was fine until we reached the junction onto the motorway.

Once we entered the motorway, it was brought to our attention that we were driving alongside, albeit briefly, a black Land Rover with blacked-out windows.

I noticed this vehicle alongside us before my husband did, and you could not see a driver. However, my husband, who likes to turn on classical FM radio while driving, could not get the radio to work at all while this vehicle was next to us. He even remarked (on noticing this vehicle himself) that it must be the Land Rover somehow blocking our signal. Significantly, as soon as he made this remark, the Land Rover sped up and moved off at speed, and the radio started to work.

Strangely, it only took us six hours to get to Folkestone in Kent from the time of setting off, and it really should have taken us at least eight hours. My husband, while finding this very odd, in the end dismissed this weird time anomaly.

On the way there, on pulling into a London-based service station, we went for a coffee and some lunch. Afterwards, I was just getting up to throw my used cup away when, as I turned around to put it in the nearby bin, in the distance I caught sight of a very pale, blond-haired man, wearing sunglasses and shorts, and he was staring at me intently, so intently in fact that for a few seconds I was unable to pull my gaze away from his! My husband came up to me then, and I was obliged to follow him back to the car park. However, before doing so, I looked back over my shoulder, but the man had gone. Nevertheless, I had studied him for long enough to take in his basic features, and this would prove to be significant later.

We holidayed in a rented cottage, and nothing out of the ordinary happened while we were in Kent.

However, towards the end of the holiday, we stopped off en route to meet up with some old friends, and booked into a Travel Inn hotel to stay overnight in order to break up our return journey.

I had a strange feeling of foreboding that night and was unable to get to sleep, even though I felt very tired.

At 1 a.m. (I know this because I checked my watch at the time) I heard an argument taking place in the room next door — at least it sounded like an argument, though I couldn't make out the words.

Ten minutes later, I was just starting to nod off when something ran at me from behind; I know this because I heard the footfalls of whatever it was, and I then felt something thud into my back. Also, I started to vibrate from head to toe, once again hearing that awful buzzing noise that I recognized from years ago. Recognizing this as a sign that I was about to be 'taken,' I went into a full-blown panic. Also, I was praying to God because this was all so frightening, and a voice in my head clearly said, and I quote: *"Your God can't help you now."* As in the past, the room seemed to pass from pitch darkness to daylight within seconds, and I woke up to bright sunlight coming in through the curtains.

On the journey back, I couldn't get what had happened out of my mind, but in the end I just tried my best to put it behind me, as past experience of this had taught me that it would do me little good telling anyone about it!

When we got back from Kent, my brother came to stay, and we went to Grasmere in the Lake District for the day.

While we were there, we all went into an elegant old hotel

garden to enjoy a cup of tea al fresco, and nothing happened until we got up to go.

As we were getting up, I noticed a thin, pale, stern-looking man who was sitting to my immediate right on a deckchair. He had short pale-blond hair and wore shorts and sunglasses, and I immediately felt that I had seen him somewhere before. His legs were free of any body hair, as were his arms, and I remember thinking that this was a bit odd, as most men are hairy, at least on their arms. As I walked past him, although my brother and my husband failed to notice him at all, he got my attention because he seemed to be staring at me intently, and he actually made me feel quite uneasy. As I looked at him, I felt as if he was trying to say once again: *"Yes, we are here!"*

Once I got to the car with my husband and brother, it came back to me where I had seen this man before. It was at the London motorway services that I had seen this same identical man during our car journey down to Kent!

Holiday in Skegness: July 7, 2021

In July of the following year, we went on holiday to Skegness and rented a cottage in a small village a few miles out from the main town. Nothing unusual happened for the first two days. However, on the Wednesday, some high strangeness occurred.

My youngest son, who has high-functioning autism, had a complete meltdown and asked if he could sleep next to his dad in our double-bedded bedroom. Therefore, I was obliged to take one of the twin beds next to my eldest son, who generally doesn't come to bed until very late on holidays, usually around 3 a.m.

So off I went to bed, and I got to sleep easily enough. In the early morning hours (I am estimating the time to be 2 a.m., as I didn't look at my watch) I woke up and glanced over at my eldest son's bed, and was reassured to see what I thought was him asleep in the bed. However, I could not make out any facial features in the dark room, and could just about make out what I assumed was a lump of son-shaped human in the opposite bed. I didn't bother to check any further, nor did I feel scared, as I assumed this was my child. I then seemed to instantly and suspiciously black out, only to be woken by my older son at 4 a.m. I know it was then because I asked him the time, and I asked why he was switching the light on.

He replied that he had only just come to bed and that he was looking for his toothbrush. I was shocked by this information and told him that I thought he was in bed two hours ago. But he insisted that he had been downstairs all the time and had only just come to bed!

I didn't tell him what a puzzling conundrum this created in my mind. It has left me wondering just why 'someone' would take the trouble to fool me into thinking that my son was in bed next to me. Was I seeing things? I genuinely believe that the shape of the 'person' resembled my son's shape, and whoever this was, they were lying on their side in bed, just as he does! So, I am now left wondering about this.

After we returned from holiday, nothing happened until the following week.

Chapter 13

Ongoing contact: As July continues, I receive another telepathic message

On Wednesday evening of July 14, 2021, I went to bed early as I had experienced a tiring day, and I soon fell asleep. I was woken at 3:10 a.m. (I know this because I glanced at my clock, which lights up in the dark) to once again find the tall silhouetted figure of a man standing in my bedroom! To say this scared me is definitely an understatement! Of course, he disappeared as soon as I scrambled to switch on my lamp.

Feeling very scared, I left a night light on and tried to get back to sleep. However, a voice in my head informed me that I would soon receive a message and to be prepared for this.

I asked how this message would be delivered, and was told: *"By one of us."*

This was all I got; no more information was forthcoming.

Later that week: Saturday July 24, 2021

On the Saturday immediately following this, I had scheduled an appointment with a local supermarket's opticians to pick up my new prescription sunglasses and my new glasses. I had been waiting for these for two weeks.

I duly went along to my appointment at 12:15, taking my son along, as he too was waiting for glasses.

The assistant dealt with me efficiently, and I put on my new sunglasses and left my son to be fitted for his, while I went along to the café to order some lunch and a latte.

While I was standing in the queue, in front of me, I noticed three very ordinary-looking people, two men and one woman. They spoke with a foreign accent, and I assumed they were Polish, as we have a lot of Polish families here in the city where

I live. I had the impression they were related to each other as well.

The strange thing about this was that the man at the very back of the group, standing close to me, was staring at me so intently that I became quite embarrassed. I assumed that he was doing this because he found me somehow attractive and was trying to make it obvious that he did.

Now let me describe these three: I didn't get a good look at the other male, but I did notice that the female in the group was very blond, with long hair and a thin athletic figure.

The man standing next to me had sandy blond hair with a slight wave; he was at least 6 feet 2 inches, and the woman would be about 5 feet 7 inches tall. He said not one word to me but persisted in staring at me intently as if he was trying to get my attention. I felt embarrassed at him staring at me for so long, and attempted a look of indifference.

Then my husband arrived to meet me for lunch, and I waved at him. The man turned around and saw my husband, and at this, all three of them, the one at the front having ordered a take-out meal, went off together, chattering and giggling.

I really thought nothing of this at all and just assumed the man at the back of the queue was being a bit forward, and frankly, cheeky.

It wasn't until I got home that I discovered that my mobile phone cover, which I swear had nothing on it when I set off on this trip, now had an inked-out set of symbols on its front cover! Now, skeptics among you will say: well, did you check your bag for any ink leaks, wet paper receipts, shopping lists, and so on? To which I can answer: yes, of course, I did a thorough search of my bag in an attempt to find a logical explanation for the inked-out symbols.

But there was nothing in my bag, and by that I mean: no leaky pens, no watery products, nothing that could have caused ink to print off onto my phone cover.

Now, you might also say that the three people at the supermarket had no connection with these things appearing, but when I thought about it afterwards, I couldn't help wondering why the man at the back of the group had stared so intently at me, without speaking one word to me. Was he attempting telepathy? I can't help wondering about this now.

It could be that these three were perfectly normal people. I will never know either way, but the energy coming off them, particularly the woman, was not normal. Suffice to say, I remain puzzled by this encounter.

See above inked-out symbols that appeared on my leather phone cover. Next to that, I have drawn the symbols on paper.

After finding the symbols, I copied them onto a piece of paper and sent them and a photo of my phone case to two UFO researchers. (See the photos included in this chapter.) These researchers were a friend of mine in Scotland who is an experiencer, and my friend the author Michel Zirger, in France.

Michel soon replied and sent me a picture of a message given to George Adamski by the Nordic human-looking ETs in the 1950s. Although my message was far smaller, the symbols on my phone cover, and the copy I reproduced (see my drawing of the symbols and the photo of my phone cover) proved to be uncannily similar to Adamski's symbols, which I obtained a copy of, but could not include in this book, due to copyright issues.

To date, I have no idea whether this is indeed the "message" I was told to expect, nor do I have any idea what it means.

My friend in Scotland sent both my photo of the phone cover and my copy of the symbols to a well-known exopolitics researcher, who drew a blank on them, stating that in his opinion they were not taken from any known Earth language and that they were definitely what he called "an unknown."

Latest experiences: late September 2021

In addition to seeing this male figure in my room in July, I feel I was taken one night during the last week of September 2021, and returned with a dark black smudge on my underwear and mattress cover. (See photos.) Just before this happened, what appeared to be a large helicopter flew overhead and I ran to the window to watch it. It had two flashing blue lights on it, and it hovered over my house at 4 a.m. for five long minutes (I know this because I timed it), for no reason that I can fathom at all.

Then I returned to bed to try to get back to sleep, but when I lay down in bed, in what seemed like a second it was morning and daylight!

The following night, the same thing happened, but there was no warning, no buzzing noise or paralysis. I just closed my eyes and it was pitch dark, then within seconds (or so it seemed) it was morning again! This is always a sign to me that I have been 'taken,' and in some ways it is more difficult to deal with than the paralysis and the buzzing that fills my body, because at least they are a signal, a warning, that something unusual is about to happen. The split-second movement from darkness to daylight really scares me, and leaves me wondering how much missing time I have lost.

Furthermore, on the second night, I woke up to find strange bird-like symbols on my hand, as if they had been pressed into there on purpose. I have no idea what this is or what it could mean.

I recently attempted to contact ETs through my meditation and music, and to my utter astonishment I did hear a woman's voice in my head. I felt that this female person was very wise and mature, perhaps even a wise elder of some sort. She told me that her name was Neharu—at least this is how it sounded. Then suddenly, I received a mental picture of her in my mind, rather as if I was watching a movie. It was detailed and she had a pear-shaped face and head that was larger than a human's. She appeared to be wearing a long dress that came high up to the neck. It seemed to give off a shimmering light when she moved. She told me that she was from a race known as "Egaroth," being from what she called the "Aldiron" system; again, I am spelling both words phonetically, and probably incorrectly.

Once we had communicated, the pictures of her faded out, but I was left amazed by this experience since this was no dream: I was fully awake when it happened, sitting in my living room on the floor. Make of that what you will.

I am frankly left amazed by this experience! It leaves me wondering if there is an ongoing plan to contact 'awake' individuals on Earth, an attempt—if you like—to wake some of us up that are actually already awake and open to further contact.

Taken to see an underground city

Just before I write my conclusion, I want to say that on rare occasions, I remember what I have seen and where I have been taken during abductions—in vivid panoramic detail. I don't know why this is. Perhaps someone forgets to erase my memory, or perhaps it is allowed.

One time only, I believe I was allowed to experience being taken as it was happening, and I will try to describe here how this felt.

One night, I had, I presume, fallen asleep, when suddenly I opened my eyes and was astounded to find myself in a huge corridor filled with ambient white light, and I could see that the walls were curved and had shiny, smooth white material on them. The atmosphere around me was warm and I was, I believe, floating along. Someone was holding me, and although I was paralyzed and feeling frightened, this someone squeezed my hand gently as if to reassure me that they meant no harm. So, we glided along, or should I say, floated fast down this long, twisting corridor.

When we got to the end of it, I could see a pale-gray sky and it was definitely daytime; so I presumed, though maybe wrongly, that we had exited a tunnel of some kind. The sky overhead was cloudless, and beneath it sat a number of very white buildings; I felt that the tallest one was some kind of temple. I attempted to get free from whoever was holding me to take a closer look, but they pulled me back and we went whizzing back down this twisting white tunnel again.

Following this, I believe I blacked out, and came to in bed in the early hours.

I have no idea where I was taken, or what I saw, but I didn't feel like this was anywhere on Earth, and I don't know how I knew that.

More recently, my family all came down with a flu bug, and we all went to the airport to have a PCR test for Covid, but they all came up negative.

However, my eldest son and my husband both went on to develop a cough, a high temperature, and a runny nose. I thought smugly that I had escaped catching this. However, on Wednesday the 29th of September, I too became ill with what felt like flu and a high temperature, and someone told me on this particular night: *"We need to take a look at you."* I actually assumed that I had dreamt this voice, and as I was aching all over and feeling very tired, I just wanted to go to sleep.

However, I then went on to have a very vivid 'dream' of being taken to a huge room, and there I was placed on some kind of bed, which seemed to adjust to my body's weight. I looked up, and a glass screen came down over me, and I could see lots of white lights stationed above other beds.

This room was enormous and I felt that I was not on Earth at all. In addition to this, whoever had taken me told me to remember to put my shoes back on, and I clearly remember doing this. These shoes were my usual gold-colored flip-flops (bedroom slippers), and I saw them in this 'dream' lined up with a number of other ordinary-looking men's and women's shoes and slippers.

I also recall seeing a lady with long fair hair standing over me, or at least this person looked female, and she seemed to be looking down at me through something. She was dressed in a tight-fitting white suit, but I could not make out her facial features at all, which was very frustrating; interestingly, this would be the case if what I was recalling was not in fact a dream, but reality, as I am near-sighted (also known as short-sighted) without my glasses! I believe that I was allowed to remember bits of this, but not all of it; and no one will change my mind on that.

Also, when I woke up, my temperature had returned to normal and I felt much better, but curiously, the first sound that I heard was what sounded like some kind of engine roaring overhead.

I ran to look out of my window, but although I could still hear this roaring engine sound receding, there was nothing to see except the early dawn sky. I stood there until the sound completely disappeared, but this is the curious thing: the sky was clear, not a cloud in it, and I could still see the moon, while the sun was just coming up over the horizon, so if it had been a plane, why couldn't I see it?

By Thursday, from feeling so ill that I couldn't walk for dizziness, I was back on my feet and typing this book!

Conclusion

There will be those who will mock me and disbelieve this account. Indeed, even members of my own family have struggled to accept what I believe I have experienced, and this is very hard for me, because when even those close to you doubt, it takes bravery to come out and share this with a wider audience.

Some years ago now, in 2008, after carrying this around for years and struggling to process what I had experienced, I contacted a fellow experiencer named Mike Oram, the British author of the book *Does It Rain in Other Dimensions?* I did this because I was feeling so desperately alone and isolated with my own experiences of ET contact. Contact in the UK is not as widely talked about or recognized as it is in the USA, and I believe that this is an unhealthy situation that needs to change.

I remember going on the train to meet Mike and his partner Fran at a nearby town, and feeling very scared. However, I needn't have worried as both of them proved to be very friendly. I found Mike to be very sympathetic about what I had experienced, and we spent all day chatting and shared lunch together.

What he gave me was reassurance that these things have not just happened to me, but have happened to him and others too, and that moreover, they continue to happen to people all over the world! I felt so much better following this meeting and no longer felt like some kind of lunatic or madwoman.

Sadly, many experiencers have still not come forward, for the same reasons as me—because of fear of mockery and persecution by narrow-minded people who cannot allow the possibility that in this vast universe in which we live there may just be others, maybe more advanced than us, even similar in appearance to us, that are reaching out to people who are open to contact.

However, thanks to the invention of social media, which has provided us with sites like Facebook, YouTube, Twitter and Reddit, there has lately been a lot more opportunity for sharing and for like-minded people to contact each other.

I personally have reached out to others on these forums, and joined groups connected with UFO contact, UFO research, and ancient ET contact, for which I believe there exists an overwhelming body of evidence.

I have also now read widely on the subject, and in the course of my reading I have learned the following things:

1. People on Earth have been contacted before, and given face-to-face help and knowledge, many thousands of years ago following a great cataclysm and vast floods. See books by Freddy Silva.
2. Other people have been abducted. See author Budd Hopkins.
3. Other people have claimed contact with Nordic ETs and others. See Budd Hopkins, Michel Zirger, and Mike Oram.

I have to emphasize that these are merely a handful of authors/ researchers that I mention here. There are many others who have written on the same subject. Indeed, there is a vast library out there to be collated on this whole area, with books too numerous to list here along with their corresponding authors, who in my own humble opinion have provided more than enough evidence to suggest that something big is definitely going on, and has been going on since the Americans tested the first atom bomb in July 1945 at Los Alamos, New Mexico!

Because of the points I have outlined in this book, I believe that there has now occurred a shift in consciousness towards this subject and that most people are now becoming more open-minded towards the idea of possible contact.

Indeed, even those who claim to *channel* ETs have been received lately with a more open mind, and these persons have not—like me, Mike, and others—ever claimed face-to-face contact. However, in common with me, they have claimed telepathic contact with ETs, and many more people are prepared to listen to their stories; so there is definitely a sea change occurring as I write this.

This is why I believed it was time to come out about my own experiences and share them with a wider audience than I had previously.

However, I do not look for fame or even fortune in doing this. That is why I have chosen not to use my usual name as author of this book, and have only used my middle Christian name, and my maiden name.

My main aim is to get my story out there, alongside other accounts that are already there. In other words, I want to make my contribution to the growing body of circumstantial evidence worldwide that extraterrestrial contact with ordinary people is indeed happening on a larger scale than we may realize.

Following the momentous events of 2008, I was accepted onto a course to train to be a teacher, and I commenced teacher training. I found this tough going and barely made it to the end of the course. However, I eventually found my ideal job; and I have since spent a number of years teaching English as a first, and as a second, language.

In addition to this, I also write poetry, and as you will note from the drawings in this book, I am also an amateur artist and a member of an art group where I live in the UK. I have exhibited my artwork locally where I live (though not my alien/ET artwork) and I am known as a local artist where I live.

These, then, are the experiences I am able to recall up to this date. There is, to me, no pattern or way of predicting when they will happen, nor do I have any confirmed reason as to why I have had so many of them. But I swear that what I have written here is the truth as I have experienced it, and I don't believe that I have exaggerated in any way.

My experiences have puzzled me beyond measure at times, and continue to fascinate and perplex me, even as I write this account.

Most of my contacts have been, thankfully, with mostly benevolent ETs, especially the 'Nordics,' and while they were a bit unnerving, they have, in a way, made me much more aware than I perhaps might have been that humans on Earth are most certainly not alone.

Perhaps they were trying to expand my consciousness and my core spiritual beliefs, which have shifted upwards, largely due to their interventions.

I would love to meet one of them and actually have a conversation.

However, some of my contacts have not been as easy, and I have frequently encountered the 'Gray' aliens, especially when I was in my teens. These encounters did not feel as benevolent or as non-threatening as those with the more human-looking 'Nordics.'

For those who think—as many no doubt do—that I, and others like me, have somehow imagined, made up, exaggerated, or invented these experiences, nothing of what I or any one of those other 'experiencers' says is going to convince them otherwise, and I am not here to convince people.

Primarily, I wanted to get my story out there, because I know for a fact that there are others like me, and it is with the primary aim of reaching out to them that I have chosen, albeit late in the day, to tell my story.

Has it been easy going through all of this and revisiting and recalling the things I have seen and experienced? To that I would answer a very firm "No!"

There are close family members who still have no knowledge of what I have been through, and moreover, I suspect that they would not understand and would think that I was, to use an old British word, going 'barmy' (crazy), were I to tell them.

There is of course the risk that they will find and read this book, but that is a risk I will have to take, because I do not feel that I can keep my story to myself any longer.

The reasons for this are numerous, but a primary one is this: In the USA, there are counselors and therapists who actively deal with abduction/experiencer scenarios. To date, I have found no one in the UK who does this!

The fact is that I have been regularly 'taken' against my will, left terrified, left with missing time, left outside my house, left feeling helpless, left with burns, strange marks, and black stains on my bedding and night attire, and left with confused, fragmented memories of meetings with what I am forced to conclude were various ETs.

However, when I tried to seek counseling about this, I was immediately threatened with being sent to a psychiatrist by the counselor I went to, and it was clear to me that she could not cope in any way or form with what I was telling her! Simply put, my experiences were completely outside her frame of reference.

I believe this has to change. It has changed in the USA, and it can change in the UK too.

So, given this, I have just recently completed an introductory course in counseling and psychotherapy, with the aim of eventually becoming a qualified therapist myself.

I often ask myself, as covered in a previous chapter, why me?

Well, another very frightening reason that I failed to mention might simply be that we are viewed by ETs as very much 'lesser than' them, particularly by what we refer to as the 'Gray' aliens.

I have to ask myself, do they view us rather in the same way as we view farmyard animals, feeling free to help themselves to the things our bodies produce? This is a very frightening thought, but if this is the case, then I believe from what I have read that someone, somewhere on Earth, has okayed it, because there are vast numbers of us who have been contacted!

For more about this particular 'rabbit hole,' I would suggest that you look up Budd Hopkins for background and theories on the 'Gray' aliens' motives for abducting citizens.

With 'disclosure,' then, should there also be an amnesty for those who have made errors of judgment in compromising the human race on Earth?

I believe there should, and I am ready to forgive, because I am, and always will be, a positive person whose beliefs hold true to the basic tenets set down in all the great world religions, and that is that it is better to forgive than to hold on to anger! Anger and bitterness will only make you ill, and that is why there is a need for understanding therapists in this area of 'high strangeness.' I know that I am not alone in being a British experiencer, and I believe that there will definitely be others just like me.

From the author

Thank you for purchasing *Phantoms in the Night or ETs? My lifelong experience of contact with the paranormal.* My sincere hope is that you derived as much from reading this book as I have in creating it. If you have a few moments, please feel free to add your review of the book to your favorite online site for feedback.

If you wish to talk to me about my book, you can reach me via email at: ditsy10@gmail.com

Appendix

My poems on realizing that I may be a 'Third Wave Volunteer' and an abductee

On Realizing That I Am Probably A 'Third Wave Volunteer'
(see Dolores Cannon in bibliography)
I asked the wind:
Why am I here?
And she replied:
Ask the sunset, her face is wide.
And the sunset gave me indigo,
And the blue sky made my eyes blink
Because I'd been used to a gentler sun...
Then I asked the Earth for green,
and felt her energy
Pass through me like a pulse,
and raise her hopeful voice.
She said: "You're here by choice!"
I said: "Am I? Am I?"
Then she said: "Thank you for coming."
And I tasted my salty tears,
And I said to the Earth: "You're welcome!"

What Abduction Feels Like At First
Now I see you,
But what am I seeing?
Time frozen,
in a moment,
Do I hear footsteps?
I cannot turn my head!

No! This is not a dream!

It is their web thickening.
As faces barely seen,
Peer at me through the dark.

And now I carry their faces in my head,
And I have to wonder what they wanted.
Because when they returned me,
To where I was,
The earth still turned on its axis,
Birds still sung,
Cars still beeped,
And cats still yowled,
Their territorial warnings,
Adding to the sing song
Of all my familiar suburban sounds.

Those sunbathed gardens,
looked so ordinary,
In the thin dawn light.
Those rose bushes,
Stood straight as sentries,
Denied that any mystery had been,
For there was no trace,
Except for some marks upon my skin,
Disputable marks,
That no one would believe.

Who?
Curious eyes that see the lights,
Watch them as they fall and sigh,
Hidden, humming across the sky,
It makes me wonder why?
Darkness clad strangers inside my room,
Standing in shadows and in gloom,

Have they come to take me home?
Talking voices since I was young,
Talking voices that rose and sung!
Leading me into the dawn fields,
Wild goose chases that never felt real.
So why do you play these games with me?
Why won't you come and let me see—you?
Dark black flashes across my eyes,
Deeper flashes of alien skies?
Down a passage of pure white,
Pulls my soul to a waiting light.
To a silent citadel, burning bright,
You pulled me back, but I wanted to,
Come nearer.
You hide your places across the land,
In shifting seas and shifting sand,
Sand that falls right through my hand,
See your craft, far away they stand,
Why did you come so close to me?
Why the savior in a foreign land?
Twisting tales I can't unravel,
Cutting my feet on your alien gravel.
In the shadows you talk to me,
Give me clues I just can't see!
I bet you're laughing, I bet you're free,
To locate me any time you please.
Hidden in a cloak of invisibility,
In a cocoon I cannot see.
Staring out of your flying citadels,
Flying dragons and sulphur smells,
Memories accumulated in a
pulsing blend of vivid, silent stills,
Chimeras in the early morn,
Silver flashes in the dawn.

Leading me on and teasing me,
Just beyond my view.

Notes

1. 39+ Smartphone Statistics You Should Know in 2020_view42. com/resources/smartphone-statistics/
2. https://yougov.co.uk/topics/science/articles-reports/2021/06/25/half-britons-think-aliens-exist-and-7-claim-have-s Eir Nolsoe, Data journalist, Science and the Environment, 25/6/21
3. https://www.nytimes.com/2021/06/25/opinion/chris-carter-aliens-ufo-xfiles.html
4. https://www.nytimes.com/2021/06/25/opinion/chris-carter-aliens-ufo-xfiles.html

Bibliography

Cannon, Delores: *The Three Waves of Volunteers and the New Earth*, Ozark Mountain Publishing, Huntsville, USA, 2011.

Hopkins, Budd: *Intruders*, Random House, New York, USA, 1987.

Hopkins, Budd/Rainey, Carol: *Sight Unseen: Science, UFO Invisibility and Transgenic Beings*, Simon and Schuster, New York, USA, 2003.

Leir, Roger, Dr.: *Alien Implants*, Dell, New York, USA, 2000.

Moody, Raymond, MD: *Coming Back*, Bantam, New York, USA, 1992.

Oram, Mike: *Does It Rain in Other Dimensions?*, John Hunt, Ropley, UK, 2007.

Rodwell, Mary: *Awakenings*, Beyond Publications, Leeds, UK, 2002.

Silva, Freddy: *The Missing Lands*, Publisher—Freddy Silva, 2019.

Stevenson, Ian: *Where Reincarnation and Biology Intersect*, Praeger, Westport, CT, USA, 1997.

Strieber, Whitley: *Communion: A True Story*, William Morrow & Co., New York, USA, 1987.

Tellinger, Michael: *Slave Species of the Gods*, Bear & Company, Rochester, VT, USA, 2012.

Tucker, Jim B., MD: *Return To Life*, St Martin's Press, New York, USA, 2013.

Wallis, Paul: *Escaping From Eden*, Axis Mundi Books, UK, 2020.

Zirger, Michel: *"We Are Here!" Visitors Without a Passport*, Amazon.com Company, 2017.

**6TH
BOOKS**

ALL THINGS PARANORMAL

Investigations, explanations and deliberations on the paranormal, supernatural, explainable or unexplainable. 6th Books seeks to give answers while nourishing the soul: whether making use of the scientific model or anecdotal and fun, but always beautifully written.
Titles cover everything within parapsychology: how to, lifestyles, alternative medicine, beliefs, myths and theories.
If you have enjoyed this book, why not tell other readers by posting a review on your preferred book site?

Recent bestsellers from 6th Books are:

The Afterlife Unveiled
What the Dead Are Telling Us About Their World!
Stafford Betty
What happens after we die? Spirits speaking through mediums
know, and they want us to know. This book unveils their world…
Paperback: 978-1-84694-496-3 ebook: 978-1-84694-926-5

Spirit Release
Sue Allen
A guide to psychic attack, curses, witchcraft, spirit attachment,
possession, soul retrieval, haunting, deliverance, exorcism and
more, as taught at the College of Psychic Studies.
Paperback: 978-1-84694-033-0 ebook: 978-1-84694-651-6

I'm Still With You
True Stories of Healing Grief Through Spirit Communication
Carole J. Obley
A series of after-death spirit communications which uplift, comfort
and heal, and show how love helps us grieve.
Paperback: 978-1-84694-107-8 ebook: 978-1-84694-639-4

Less Incomplete
A Guide to Experiencing the Human Condition Beyond the
Physical Body
Sandie Gustus
Based on 40 years of scientific research, this book is a dynamic
guide to understanding life beyond the physical body.
Paperback: 978-1-84694-351-5 ebook: 978-1-84694-892-3

Advanced Psychic Development
Becky Walsh
Learn how to practise as a professional, contemporary spiritual medium.
Paperback: 978-1-84694-062-0 ebook: 978-1-78099-941-8

Astral Projection Made Easy
and overcoming the fear of death
Stephanie June Sorrell
From the popular Made Easy series, *Astral Projection Made Easy* helps to eliminate the fear of death, through discussion of life beyond the physical body.
Paperback: 978-1-84694-611-0 ebook: 978-1-78099-225-9

The Miracle Workers Handbook
Seven Levels of Power and Manifestation of the Virgin Mary
Sherrie Dillard
Learn how to invoke the Virgin Mary's presence, communicate with her, receive her grace and miracles and become a miracle worker.
Paperback: 978-1-84694-920-3 ebook: 978-1-84694-921-0

Divine Guidance
The Answers You Need to Make Miracles
Stephanie J. King
Ask any question and the answer will be presented, like a direct line to higher realms... *Divine Guidance* helps you to regain control over your own journey through life.
Paperback: 978-1-78099-794-0 ebook: 978-1-78099-793-3

The End of Death
How Near-Death Experiences Prove the Afterlife
Admir Serrano
A compelling examination of the phenomena of Near-Death Experiences.
Paperback: 978-1-78279-233-8 ebook: 978-1-78279-232-1

Where After
Mariel Forde Clarke
A journey that will compel readers to view life after death in a completely different way.
Paperback: 978-1-78904-617-5 ebook: 978-1-78904-618-2

Harvest: The True Story of Alien Abduction
G. L. Davies
G. L. Davies's most terrifying investigation yet reveals one woman's terrifying ordeal of alien visitation, nightmarish visions and a prophecy of destruction on a scale never before seen in Pembrokeshire's peaceful history.
Paperback: 978-1-78904-385-3 ebook: 978-1-78904-386-0

The Scars of Eden
Paul Wallis
How do we distinguish between our ancestors' ideas of God and close encounters of an extra-terrestrial kind?
Paperback: 978-1-78904-852-0 ebook: 978-1-78904-853-7

Readers of ebooks can buy or view any of these bestsellers by clicking on the live link in the title. Most titles are published in paperback and as an ebook. Paperbacks are available in traditional bookshops. Both print and ebook formats are available online.
Find more titles and sign up to our readers' newsletter at http://www.johnhuntpublishing.com/mind-body-spirit.
Follow us on Facebook at https://www.facebook.com/OBooks and Twitter at https://twitter.com/obooks.